In my formative years as a you[...] [...]f
the fact that I faced many ch[...] d
behaviour. Few writers helped me to understand how I should
respond to these challenges and think and live as a Christian as much
as John Stott did. The challenges of faithfulness to God's way are
more acute and complex today than when I was a young Christian.
In these little books, you find the essence of Stott's thinking about
the Christian life; it is refreshing to read this material again and see
how relevant and health-giving it is for today. I'm grateful to Inter-
Varsity Press and to Tim Chester for making Stott's thinking
accessible to a new generation.

Ajith Fernando, Teaching Director, Youth for Christ, Sri Lanka

Technology has enabled more voices to clamour for our attention
than ever before, while, at the same time, people's ability to listen
carefully seems to have deteriorated as never before. John Stott's
speaking and writing was renowned for two things in particular: he
taught us how to listen attentively to God in order to live faithfully
for God; and he modelled how to listen to the world sensitively in
order to communicate God's purposes intelligibly. He taught us to
listen. That is why it is such a thrill to see *The Contemporary Christian*
carefully revived in a new format as a series for a new generation of
readers. As we read, may we listen well!

Mark Meynell, Director (Europe and Caribbean) Langham
Preaching, Langham Partnership and author of *Cross-Examined*
and *When Darkness Seems My Closest Friend*

It is always refreshing, enlightening and challenging reading from
the pen of John Stott. I am totally delighted that one of his most
significant works will continue to be available, hopefully for more
decades to come. The way Stott strives to be faithful to the Word of
God and relevant to his world – secularized Western society – as the
locus for the drama of God's action, is exemplary, especially for those

of us ordained to the service of the church in our diverse contexts. I highly commend The Contemporary Christian series to all who share the same pursuit – listening intently to God's Word and God's world, hearing and obeying God.

David Zac Niringiye, author of *The Church: God's Pilgrim People*

I am delighted that a new generation will now be able to benefit from this rich teaching, which so helped me when it first appeared. As always with John Stott, there is a wonderful blend of faithful exposition of the Bible, rigorous engagement with the world and challenging applications for our lives.

Vaughan Roberts, Rector, St Ebbe's Church, Oxford, and author of a number of books, including *God's Big Picture* (IVP)

Imagine being like a child overwhelmed by hundreds of jigsaw puzzle pieces – you just can't put them together! And then imagine that a kindly old uncle comes along and helps you to assemble the whole thing, piece by piece. That is what it felt like reading John Stott's book *The Contemporary Christian*. For those of us who feel we can't get our heads around our Bibles, let alone our world, he comes along and, with his staggering gifts of clarity and insight, helps us, step by step, to work out what it means to understand our world through biblical lenses. It's then a great blessing to have Tim Chester's questions at the end of each chapter, which help us to think through and internalize each step.

Rico Tice, Senior Minister for Evangelism, All Souls, Langham Place, London, and co-author of *Christianity Explored*

I have long benefited from the work of John Stott because of the way he combines rigorous engagement of the biblical text and careful engagement with the culture of his day. The Contemporary Christian series presents Stott at his very best. It displays his commitment to biblical authority, his zeal for the mission of the church and his call to faithful witness in the world. Stott's reflections here are a must-read for church leaders today.

Trevin Wax, Director of Bibles and Reference, LifeWay Christian Resources, and author of *This Is Our Time* and *Eschatological Discipleship*

The Contemporary Christian

THE DISCIPLE

A Calling to Be Christlike

John Stott with Tim Chester

INTER-VARSITY PRESS
36 Causton Street, London SW1P 4ST, England
Email: ivp@ivpbooks.com
Website: www.ivpbooks.com

This volume has been adapted from John Stott, *The Contemporary Christian* (1992), and is one of five titles published in this format in The Contemporary Christian series, with extra text, including questions, by Tim Chester.

Unless otherwise indicated, Scripture quotations are taken from the Holy Bible, New International Version (Anglicized edition). Copyright © 1979, 1984, 2011 by Biblica. Used by permission of Hodder & Stoughton Ltd, an Hachette UK company. All rights reserved. 'NIV' is a registered trademark of Biblica. UK trademark number 1448790.

Scripture quotations marked AV are taken from the Authorized Version of the Bible (The King James Bible), the rights in which are vested in the Crown, and are reproduced by permission of the Crown's patentee, Cambridge University Press.

Scripture quotations marked GNT are taken from the Good News Translation® (Today's English Version, Second Edition), formerly called the Good News Bible. Copyright © 1992 by the American Bible Society. All rights reserved.

Scripture quotations marked NEB are from the New English Bible, copyright © The Delegates of the the Oxford University Press and The Syndics of Cambridge University Press, 1961, 1970. Used by permission.

Scripture quotations marked RSV are taken from the Revised Standard Version of the Bible, copyright © 1946, 1952, 1971 by the Division of Christian Education of the National Council of the Churches of Christ in the United States of America. Used by permission. All rights reserved.

The Scripture quotation marked RV is taken from the Revised Version of the Bible (1885).

British Library Cataloguing-in-Publication Data
A catalogue record for this book is available from the British Library.

ISBN: 978-1-78359-930-1
eBook ISBN: 978-1-78359-931-8

Set in Minion

Typeset in Great Britain by CRB Associates, Potterhanworth, Lincolnshire
Print and production managed in Great Britain by Jellyfish Print Solutions

Inter-Varsity Press publishes Christian books that are true to the Bible and that communicate the gospel, develop discipleship and strengthen the church for its mission in the world.

IVP originated within the Inter-Varsity Fellowship, now the Universities and Colleges Christian Fellowship, a student movement connecting Christian Unions in universities and colleges throughout Great Britain, and a member movement of the International Fellowship of Evangelical Students. Website: www.uccf.org.uk. That historic association is maintained, and all senior IVP staff and committee members subscribe to the UCCF Basis of Faith.

Contents

About the authors

John Stott had a worldwide ministry as a church leader, a Bible expositor and the author of many award-winning books. He was Rector Emeritus of All Souls, Langham Place, London, and Founder-President of the Langham Partnership.

Tim Chester is Pastor of Grace Church, Boroughbridge, North Yorkshire, Chair of Keswick Ministries and the author of more than forty books.

Preface

To be 'contemporary' is to live in the present, and to move with the times, without worrying too much about the past or the future.

To be a 'contemporary Christian', however, is to live in a present that is enriched by our knowledge of the past and by our expectation of the future. Our Christian faith demands this. Why? Because the God we trust and worship is 'the Alpha and the Omega . . . who is, and who was, and who is to come, the Almighty',[1] while the Jesus Christ we follow is 'the same yesterday and today and for ever'.[2]

So this book and series are about how Christians handle time – how we can bring the past, the present and the future together in our thinking and living. Two main challenges face us. The first is the tension between the 'then' (past) and the 'now' (present), and the second the tension between the 'now' (present) and the 'not yet' (future).

The Introduction opens up the first problem. Is it possible for us truly to honour the past and live in the present at the same time? Can we preserve Christianity's historic identity intact, without cutting ourselves off from those around us? Can we communicate the gospel in ways that are exciting and modern, without distorting or even destroying it? Can we be authentic and fresh at the same time, or do we have to choose?

The Conclusion opens up the second problem: the tension between the 'now' and the 'not yet'. How far can we explore and experience everything that God has said and done through Christ, without straying into what has not yet been revealed or given? How can we develop a proper sense of humility about a future yet to unfold, without becoming complacent about where we are in the present?

In between these enquiries into the influences of the past and the future comes an exploration about our Christian responsibilities in the present.

This series is about questions of doctrine and discipleship under the five headings: 'The Gospel', 'The Disciple' (the book you are holding in your hands), 'The Bible', 'The Church' and 'The World', though I make no attempt to be systematic, let alone exhaustive.

In addition to the topic of time, and the relations between past, present and future, there is a second theme running through this series: the need for us to talk less and listen more.

I believe we are called to the difficult and even painful task of 'double listening'. We are to listen carefully (although of course with differing degrees of respect) both to the ancient Word and to the modern world, in order to relate the one to the other with a combination of faithfulness and sensitivity.

Each book in this series is an attempt at double listening. It is my firm conviction that, if we can only develop our capacity for double listening, we will avoid the opposite pitfalls of unfaithfulness and irrelevance, and truly be able to speak God's Word to God's world with effectiveness today.

Adapted from the original Preface by John Stott in 1991

A note to the reader

The original book entitled *The Contemporary Christian*, on which this volume and series are based, may not seem 'contemporary' to readers more than a quarter of a century later. But both the publisher and John Stott's Literary Executors are convinced that the issues which John Stott addresses in this book are every bit as relevant today as when they were first written.

The question was how to make this seminal work accessible for new generations of readers. We have sought to do this in the following ways:

- The original work has been divided into a series of several smaller volumes based on the five major sections of the original.
- Words that may not resonate with the twenty-first-century reader have been updated, while great care has been taken to maintain the thought process and style of the author in the original.
- Each chapter is now followed by questions from a current bestselling Christian author to aid reflection and response.

Lovers of the original work have expressed delight that this book is being made available in a way that extends its reach and influence well into a new century. We pray that your life will be enriched as you read, as the lives of many have already been greatly enriched by the original edition.

Series introduction
The Contemporary Christian:
the then and the now

The expression 'the contemporary Christian' strikes many as a contradiction in terms. Isn't Christianity an antique relic from the remote past, irrelevant to people in today's world?

My purpose in this series is to show that there is such a thing as 'contemporary Christianity' – not something newfangled, but original, historic, orthodox, biblical Christianity sensitively related to the modern world.

Christianity: both historical and contemporary

We begin by reaffirming that Christianity is a historical religion. Of course, every religion arose in a particular historical context. Christianity, however, makes an especially strong claim to be historical because it rests not only on a historical *person*, Jesus of Nazareth, but on certain historical *events* which involved him, especially his birth, death and resurrection. There is a common thread here with the Judaism from which Christianity sprang. The Old Testament presents God not only as 'the God of Abraham, Isaac and Jacob', but also as the God of the covenant that he made with Abraham, and then renewed with Isaac and Jacob. Again, he is not only 'the God of Moses', but is also seen as the Redeemer responsible for the exodus, who went on to renew the covenant yet again at Mount Sinai.

Christians are forever tethered in heart and mind to these decisive, historical events of the past. We are constantly encouraged in the

Bible to look back to them with thankfulness. Indeed, God deliberately made provision for his people to recall his saving actions on a regular basis. Supremely, the Lord's Supper or Holy Communion enables us to call the atoning death of Christ regularly to mind and so bring the past into the present.

But the problem is that Christianity's foundational events took place such a long time ago. I had a conversation with two brothers some years ago – students who told me they had turned away from the faith of their parents. One was now an agnostic, the other an atheist. I asked why. Did they no longer believe in the truth of Christianity? No, their dilemma was not whether Christianity was *true*, but whether it was *relevant*. How could it be? Christianity, they went on, was a primitive, Palestinian religion from long ago. So what on earth did it have to offer them, living in the exciting, modern world?

This view of Christianity is widespread. The world has changed dramatically since Jesus' day, and goes on changing with ever more bewildering speed. People reject the gospel, not necessarily because they think it false, but because it no longer resonates with them.

In response to this we need to be clear about the basic Christian conviction that God continues to speak through what he has spoken. His Word is not a prehistoric fossil, but a living message for the contemporary world. Even granted the historical particularities of the Bible and the immense complexities of the modern world, there is still a fundamental correspondence between them. God's Word remains a lamp to our feet and a light for our path.[1]

At the same time, our dilemma remains. Can Christianity both retain its authentic identity *and* demonstrate its relevance?

The desire to present Jesus in a way that appeals to our own generation is obviously right. This was the preoccupation of the German pastor Dietrich Bonhoeffer while in prison during World War 2: 'What is bothering me incessantly,' he wrote, 'is the question . . . who

2

Christ really is for us today?'[2] It is a difficult question. In answering it, the church has tended in every generation to develop images of Christ which deviate from the portrait painted by the New Testament authors.

Attempting to modernize Jesus

Here are some of the church's many attempts to present a contemporary picture of Christ, some of which have been more successful than others in remaining loyal to the original.

I think first of *Jesus the ascetic*, who inspired generations of monks and hermits. He was much like John the Baptist, for he too dressed in a camel's hair cloak, wore sandals or went barefoot, and munched locusts with evident relish. But it would be hard to reconcile this portrait with his contemporaries' criticism that he was a party-goer who 'came eating and drinking'.[3]

Then there was *Jesus the pale Galilean*. The apostate emperor Julian tried to reinstate Rome's pagan gods after Constantine had replaced them with the worship of Christ, and is reported as having said on his deathbed in AD 363, 'You have conquered, O Galilean.' His words were popularized by the nineteenth-century poet Swinburne:

Thou hast conquered, O pale Galilean;
The world has grown grey from thy breath.

This image of Jesus was perpetuated in medieval art and stained glass, with a heavenly halo and a colourless complexion, eyes lifted to the sky and feet never quite touching the ground.

In contrast to the presentations of Jesus as weak, suffering and defeated, there was *Jesus the cosmic Christ*, much loved by the Byzantine church leaders. They depicted him as the King of kings and Lord of lords, the creator and ruler of the universe. Yet, exalted high above all things, glorified and reigning, he seemed aloof from

3

the real world, and even from his own humanity, as revealed in the incarnation and the cross.

At the opposite end of the theological spectrum, the seventeenth- and eighteenth-century deists of the Enlightenment constructed in their own image *Jesus the teacher of common sense*,[4] entirely human and not divine at all. The most dramatic example is the work of Thomas Jefferson, President of the United States from 1801 to 1809. Rejecting the supernatural as incompatible with reason, he produced his own edition of the Gospels, in which all miracles and mysteries were systematically eliminated. What is left is a guide to a merely human moral teacher.

In the twentieth century we were presented with a wide range of options. Two of the best known owe their popularity to musicals. There is *Jesus the clown* of *Godspell*, who spends his time singing and dancing, and thus captures something of the gaiety of Jesus, but hardly takes his mission seriously. Somewhat similar is *Jesus Christ Superstar*, the disillusioned celebrity, who once thought he knew who he was, but in Gethsemane was no longer sure.

The late President of Cuba, Fidel Castro, frequently referred to Jesus as 'a great revolutionary', and there have been many attempts to portray him as *Jesus the freedom fighter*, the urban guerrilla, the first-century Che Guevara, with black beard and flashing eyes, whose most characteristic gesture was to overthrow the tables of the moneychangers and to drive them out of the temple with a whip.

These different portraits illustrate the recurring tendency to update Christ in line with current fashions. It began in the apostolic age, with Paul needing to warn of false teachers who were preaching 'a Jesus other than the Jesus we [apostles] preached'.[5] Each succeeding generation tends to read back into him its own ideas and hopes, and create him in its own image.

Their motive is right (to paint a contemporary portrait of Jesus), but the result is always distorted (as the portrait is unauthentic). The challenge before us is to present Jesus to our generation in ways that are both accurate and appealing.

Calling for double listening

The main reason for every betrayal of the authentic Jesus is that we pay too much attention to contemporary trends and too little to God's Word. The thirst for relevance becomes so demanding that we feel we have to give in to it, whatever the cost. We become slaves to the latest fad, prepared to sacrifice truth on the altar of modernity. The quest for relevance degenerates into a lust for popularity. For the opposite extreme to irrelevance is accommodation, a feeble-minded, unprincipled surrender to the spirit of the time.

God's people live in a world which can be actively hostile. We are constantly exposed to the pressure to conform.

Thank God, however, that there have always been those who have stood firm, sometimes alone, and refused to compromise. I think of Jeremiah in the sixth century BC, and Paul in his day ('everyone . . . has deserted me'),[6] Athanasius in the fourth century and Luther in the sixteenth.

In our own day, we too need to resolve to present the biblical gospel in such a way as to speak to modern dilemmas, fears and frustrations, but with equal determination not to compromise it in so doing. Some stumbling-blocks are intrinsic to the original gospel and cannot be eliminated or soft-pedalled in order to make it easier to accept. The gospel contains some features so alien to modern thought that it will always appear foolish, however hard we strive to show that it is 'true and reasonable'.[7] The cross will always be an assault on human self-righteousness and a challenge to human self-indulgence. Its 'scandal' (stumbling-block) simply cannot be removed. The church speaks most authentically not when it has become indistinguishable from the world around us, but when its distinctive light shines most brightly.

However keen we are to communicate God's Word to others, we must be faithful to that Word and, if necessary, be prepared to suffer for it. God's word to Ezekiel encourages us: 'Do not be afraid of them . . . You must speak my words to them, whether they listen or fail to listen, for they are rebellious.'[8] Our calling is to be faithful and relevant, not merely trendy.

How, then, can we develop a Christian mind which is both shaped by the truths of historic, biblical Christianity and also fully immersed in the realities of the contemporary world? We have to begin with a double refusal. We refuse to become either so absorbed in the Word that we *escape* into it and fail to let it confront the world, or so absorbed in the world that we *conform* to it and fail to subject it to the judgment of the Word.

In place of this double refusal, we are called to double listening. We need to listen to the Word of God with expectancy and humility, ready for God perhaps to confront us with a word that may be disturbing and uninvited. And we must also listen to the world around us. The voices we hear may take the form of shrill and strident protest. There will also be the anguished cries of those who are suffering, and the pain, doubt, anger, alienation and even despair of those who are at odds with God. We listen to the Word with humble reverence, anxious to understand it, and resolved to believe and obey what we come to understand. We listen to the world with critical alertness, anxious to understand it too, and resolved not necessarily to believe and obey it, but to sympathize with it and to seek grace to discover how the gospel relates to it.

Everybody finds listening difficult. But are Christians sometimes less good at listening than others? We can learn from the so-called 'comforters' in the Old Testament book of Job. They began well. When they heard about Job's troubles, they came to visit him and, seeing how great his sufferings were, said nothing to him for a whole week. If only they had continued as they began, and kept their mouths shut! Instead, they trotted out their conventional view – that every sinner suffers for his own sins – in the most insensitive way. They did not really listen to what Job had to say. They merely repeated their own thoughtless and heartless claptrap, until in the end God stepped in and rebuked them for having misrepresented him.

We need to cultivate 'double listening', the ability to listen to two voices at the same time – the voice of God through the Bible and the voices of men and women around us. These voices will often contradict one another, but our purpose in listening to them both is to discover how they relate to each other. Double listening is indispensable to Christian discipleship and to Christian mission.

It is only through this discipline of double listening that it is possible to become a 'contemporary Christian'. We bring 'historical' and 'contemporary' together as we learn to apply the Word to the world, proclaiming good news that is both true and new.

To put it in a nutshell, we live in the 'now' in the light of the 'then'.

The Disciple
Introduction

Christian discipleship (that is, following Christ) is a many-faceted responsibility. The four aspects I have chosen could appear somewhat random, but all of them tend to be underrated or even overlooked.

I begin with 'The listening ear'. For, although all our bodily organs are to be consecrated to God (including our eyes and lips, our hands and feet), a good case can be made for seeing our ears as the most important. Every true disciple is a listener, as we began to see in the Series introduction.

Chapter 2 ('Mind and emotions') recalls that our Creator has made us both rational and emotional persons, and then it explores some of the more significant links between these two features of the human personality.

In chapter 3, under the title 'Guidance, vocation and ministry', we discover that discipleship implies service, and consider how we can discern the will of God and the call of God in our lives.

For the final chapter is reserved a discussion of the first fruit of the Spirit, which is love. Its primacy in Christian disciples is well expressed in the Book of Common Prayer, which describes it as 'that most excellent gift of charity, the very bond of peace and of all virtues, without which whosoever liveth is counted dead before God'.

1

The listening ear

We've already noted that one of the most important – and much-neglected – ingredients of Christian discipleship is the cultivation of a listening ear. Bad listeners do not make good disciples.

The apostle James was clear about this. His warnings that the tongue is 'a restless evil, full of deadly poison'[1] are well known, but he has no comparable criticism of the ear. He urges us not to talk too much, but seems to suggest that we can never listen too much. Here is his exhortation: 'My dear brothers and sisters, take note of this: everyone should be quick to listen, slow to speak and slow to become angry, because human anger does not produce the righteousness that God desires.'[2]

What a remarkable organ God has created in the form of the human ear! Of course, what we usually call the ear is only the *outer ear*, that fleshy projection on the side of the head which comes in a variety of shapes and sizes. From it a two-centimetre canal leads to the eardrum, behind which is the *middle ear*. Here the body's three tiniest bones (popularly known as the anvil, the hammer and the stirrup) amplify sound twenty-two times and pass it on to the *inner ear*, where the real hearing takes place. Its main component is the snail-shaped tube named the cochlea. It contains thousands of microscopic, hair-like cells, each of which is tuned to one particular vibration. The vibrations are now converted into electric impulses, which convey sound to the brain for decoding along 30,000 circuits of the auditory nerve, enough for a sizeable city's telephone service. The human ear has rightly been celebrated as 'a triumph of miniaturization'.[3]

When you think how versatile and sensitive this organ is, it is a great pity that we do not put it to better use and develop our capacity for listening. I am thinking not only of music, birdsong and animal calls, but also of the value of conversation for our relationships. Involuntary deafness is a grievous disability; deliberate deafness is both a sin and a folly.

This is one of the main themes of Alan Parker's film *Birdy*, which is based on William Wharton's novel. Its key statement is the throwaway line near the end that 'nobody listens to anybody any longer'. The film depicts the friendship of two adolescent boys in Philadelphia, Al and Birdy, which blossoms in spite of Birdy's weird obsession with bird flight. Drafted to Vietnam, they are both blown up. Al has to have surgery on his disfigured face, while Birdy is damaged psychologically. He retreats into impenetrable silence, and is committed to a mental hospital. He cowers in his cell like a caged bird, constantly looking up at the barred window, dreaming of escape. The two men urgently need each other's support in the cruel aftermath of war, but they cannot communicate. At last, however, the breakthrough takes place, and their friendship is restored. But the background to it is a hostile world in which people are out of touch with each other – an unsympathetic mother, an un-comprehending girlfriend, a bloody and senseless war, and a psychotherapist who lacks insight and compassion. Al and Birdy are now listening to each other again, but they seem to be the exceptions in a world in which 'nobody listens to anybody any longer'.

James's appeal to us to be 'quick to listen' is not one we find easy to follow. Many of us are compulsive talkers, especially preachers! We prefer to talk than listen, to volunteer information than confess our ignorance, to criticize than receive criticism. But who am I to be saying these things? I myself have been as great an offender in this area as anybody. Here's an example. It might seem a small incident, but it has proved to be formative for me. It was Monday morning in London, the All Souls church staff team had gathered for our weekly meeting, and I was in the chair. The others were carrying on about something which did not particularly interest me (I now forget what it was), and I am ashamed to say that I had switched off. Suddenly Ted Schroder, who might not unfairly be described at that time as 'a brash young colonial from New Zealand', and who is now a close and valued friend, blurted out, 'John, you're not listening!' I blushed. For he was quite right, and it is intolerably rude not to listen when somebody is speaking. Moreover, the tensions that were surfacing in our staff team at that time were largely due to my failure to listen. So I repented, and have many times since prayed for grace to be a better listener.

To whom, then, shall we listen? First and foremost to God.

Listening to God

One of the distinctive truths about the God of the Bible is that he is a speaking God. Unlike lifeless idols which are dumb, the living God has spoken and continues to speak. They have mouths but do not speak; he has no mouth (because he is spirit), yet speaks. And since God speaks, we must listen. This is a constant theme of the Old Testament in all three of its main sections. Take the Law: 'love the LORD your God, listen to his voice.'[4] And the wisdom literature in the Writings: 'To-day, Oh that ye would hear his voice!'[5] There are also many examples in the Prophets. For instance, Israel's 'stubbornness' of heart, of which God kept complaining to Jeremiah, consists in the fact that they 'refuse to listen to my words'.[6] The tragedy of this situation is that what constituted Israel as a special and distinct people was precisely that God had spoken to her and called her. Yet she neither listened nor responded. The result was judgment: 'When I called, they did not listen; so when they called, I would not listen.'[7] One might almost say that the epitaph engraved on the nation's tombstone was: 'The Lord God spoke to his people, but they refused to listen.' So then God sent his Son, saying, 'They will listen to my Son.' But instead they killed him.

Still today God speaks, although there is some disagreement in the church as to how he does so. I do not myself believe that he speaks to us directly and audibly, as he did for example to Abraham,[8] to the boy Samuel[9] or to Saul of Tarsus outside Damascus.[10] Nor should we claim that he addresses us 'face to face, as one speaks to a friend',[11] since this intimate relationship which God had with Moses is specifically said to have been unique.[12] To be sure, Christ's sheep know the Good Shepherd's voice and follow him,[13] for this is essential to our discipleship. But we are not promised that his voice will be audible.

What, then, about indirect utterances of God through prophets? We should certainly reject any claim that there are prophets today comparable to the biblical prophets. For they were the 'mouth' of God, special organs of revelation, whose teaching belongs to the foundation on which the church is built.[14] There may well, however, be a prophetic gift of a secondary kind, as when God gives some people special insight into his Word and his will. But we should not ascribe infallibility to such communications. Instead, we should evaluate both the character and the message of those who claim to speak from God.[15]

The principal way in which God speaks to us today is through Scripture, as the church in every generation has recognized. The words that God spoke through the biblical authors, which he caused in his providence to be written and preserved, are not a dead letter. One of the special ministries of the Holy Spirit is to make God's written Word 'alive and active' and 'sharper than any double-edged sword'.[16] So we must never separate the Word from the Spirit or the Spirit from the Word, for the simple reason that the Word of God is 'the sword of the Spirit',[17] the chief weapon he uses to accomplish his purpose in his people's lives. It is this confidence that enables us to think of Scripture as both written text and as living message. So Jesus could ask, 'What is written?'[18] and, 'Have you never read?',[19] while Paul could ask, 'What does Scripture say?',[20] almost personifying it. In other words, Scripture (which means the written Word) can be either read or listened to, and what it says is what God says through it. Through his ancient Word, God addresses the modern world. He speaks through what he has spoken.

And God calls us to listen to what 'the Spirit says to the churches' through Scripture.[21] The tragedy is that still today, as in Old Testament days, people often do not, cannot or will not listen to God. The non-communication between God and us is not because God is either dead or silent, but because we are not listening. If we are cut off during a telephone conversation, we do not jump to the conclusion that the person at the other end has died. No, it is the line which has gone dead.

Christians, too, can often become cut off from God. Is this not the main cause of the spiritual stagnation we sometimes experience? We have stopped listening to God. Perhaps we no longer have a daily quiet time of Bible reading and prayer. Or if we continue to do so, perhaps it is more a routine than a reality, because we are no longer expecting God to speak. We need, then, to adopt the attitude of Samuel and say, 'Speak, LORD, for your servant is listening.'[22] Like the servant of the Lord we should be able to say, 'He wakens me morning by morning, wakens my ear to listen like one being instructed.'[23] We should imitate Mary of Bethany who 'sat at the Lord's feet listening to what he said'.[24] Of course, we have to be active as well as contemplative, to work as well as pray, to be Marthas as well as Marys. But have we allowed the Martha in us to crowd out the Mary? Have we neglected what Jesus called the 'better' option?[25]

Listening to one another

In this second sphere of listening, the principle is clear: community depends on communication. It is only when we speak and listen to one another that our relationships develop and mature. When we stop listening to each other, relationships fall apart. There is a heavy emphasis in the book of Proverbs on the necessity and value of mutual listening. For example, 'The way of fools seems right to them, but the wise listen to advice.'[26] Similarly, 'Whoever heeds life-giving correction will be at home among the wise.'[27] Again, 'The heart of the discerning acquires knowledge, for the ears of the wise seek it out.'[28] Here, then, are exhortations to listen to advice, rebuke and instruction, together with the statement that those who do so are wise. Moreover, this need to listen applies in every sphere of life, including the home, the workplace, the state and the church.

First, it applies to *the home*. I almost feel the need to apologize for saying something so traditional, but children and young people need to listen to their parents. 'Listen, my son, to your father's instruction, and do not forsake your mother's teaching.'[29] The fact is that parents have more experience, and therefore usually more wisdom, than their offspring tend to give them credit for. Mark Twain had the candour to admit this. 'When I was a boy of fourteen,' he said, 'my father was so ignorant I could hardly stand to have the old man around. But when I got to be twenty-one, I was astonished at how much he had learned in seven years!'[30]

But if children need to listen to their parents, parents need to be humble enough to listen to their children, or they will never understand their problems. For the world in which their children are growing up is vastly different from the world of their own youth. Only patient, mutual listening can bridge the generation gap.

Next, husband and wife need to listen to one another. Marriage breakdown is nearly always preceded by communication breakdown. For whatever reason (neglect, fatigue, self-centredness or pressure of business), husband and wife are no longer taking time to listen to each other. So they drift apart, and misunderstandings, suspicions, grievances and resentments increase, until it is too late – although in fact it is never too late to start listening again.

Second, listening is essential in *the workplace*. This seems to be widely recognized, as the art of listening is now included in books and seminars on business management. For example, in *The Language of Effective Listening*, Arthur Robertson says that 'effective listening is the number one communication skill requisite to success in your professional and personal life'.[31]

Listening is especially important in conflict situations. Whenever there is a dispute in the workplace, it is almost certain that both sides have a reasonable case. Neither side is totally selfish or totally crazy. The essence of conciliation, therefore, is to persuade each side to listen to the other. Only when both sides are willing to sit down together, put aside their prejudiced positions and listen, does any possibility of reconciliation emerge.

Third, the same principle is applicable to *the state.* If democracy is government with the consent of the governed, then the governed have to be heard. Otherwise, they cannot be deemed to have given their consent. In 1864, shortly before the end of the American Civil War and before Congress's adoption of the Thirteenth Amendment abolishing slavery, Harriet Beecher Stowe interviewed Abraham Lincoln and wrote, 'Surrounded by all sorts of conflicting claims, by traitors, by half-hearted timid men, by Border States men and Free States men, by radical Abolitionists and Conservatives, Lincoln has listened to all, weighed the words of all . . .'[32] The willingness to listen to all shades of opinion is an indispensable feature of true statesmanship.

Fourth, it is true in *the church.* Church history has been a long and somewhat dismal record of controversy. Usually important theological issues have been at stake. But, as often as not, they have been exacerbated by an unwillingness or inability to listen. I myself have tried never to engage in theological debate without first listening to the other person, or reading what he or she has written, or preferably both. Of course, disagreement cannot always be overcome by dialogue, but at least our misunderstanding is diminished and our integrity preserved.

This is even more so in the case of debates among evangelical Christians. When we stay apart, and our only contact is to lob hand grenades at one another across a demilitarized zone, a caricature of one's 'opponent' develops in one's mind, complete with horns, hooves and tail! But when we meet, sit together and begin to listen, it becomes evident that our opponents are not demons after all, but normal human beings, even sisters and brothers in Christ. Then the possibility of mutual understanding and respect grows. More than this: when we listen not only to what others are saying, but to what lies *behind* what they are saying, and in particular to what it is that they are so anxious to safeguard, we often find that we want to safeguard the same thing ourselves.[33]

I am not claiming that this discipline is easy. Far from it. Listening with patient integrity to both sides of an argument can cause acute mental pain. It involves internalizing the debate until you not only grasp but *feel* the strength of both positions. Yet this is another aspect of the 'double listening' for which I am pleading in this series of books.

It is perhaps especially to pastors that God has committed the ministry of listening. Dietrich Bonhoeffer wrote of it with his customary insight:

The first service that one owes to others in the fellowship consists in listening to them. Just as love to God begins with listening to his Word, so the beginning of love for the brethren is learning to listen to them. It is God's love for us that he not only gives us his Word but also lends us his ear. So it is his work that we do for our brother when we learn to listen to him. Christians, especially ministers, so often think they must always contribute something when they are in the company of others, that this is the one service they have to render. They forget that listening can be a greater service than speaking . . .

Brotherly pastoral care is essentially distinguished from preaching by the fact that, added to the task of speaking the Word, there is the obligation of listening. There is a kind of listening with half an ear that presumes already to know what the other person has to say. It is an impatient, inattentive listening, that despises the brother, and is only waiting for a chance to speak and thus get rid of the other person. This is no fulfilment of our obligation . . . Christians have forgotten that the ministry of listening has been committed to them by him who is himself the great listener and whose work they should share. We should listen with the ears of God that we may speak the Word of God.[34]

Listening to the world

The contemporary world is positively reverberating with cries of anger, frustration and pain. Too often, however, we turn a deaf ear to these anguished voices.

First, there is the pain of those who have never heard the name of Jesus or, having heard of him, have not yet come to him. In their alienation and lostness they are hurting dreadfully. Our habit as evangelicals is to rush in with the gospel, to climb on our soapbox, and to declaim our message with little regard for the cultural situation or felt needs of the people concerned. As a result, more often than we would like to admit, we put people off, and even increase their alienation, because the way we present Christ is insensitive, clumsy and even irrelevant. Truly, 'To answer before listening – that is folly and shame.'[35]

It is better to listen before we speak, to seek to enter into the thoughts and feelings of others, to struggle to grasp their objections to the gospel, and only then to share the good news of Jesus Christ in a way that speaks to their need. This humble, searching, challenging activity is rightly called 'contextualization'. But it is essential to add that to contextualize the gospel is not in any way to manipulate it. Authentic evangelism necessitates 'double listening'. For Christian witnesses stand between the Word and the world with an obligation to listen to both, as we began to see in the Introduction.

We listen to the Word to discover ever more of the riches of Christ. And we listen to the world to discern which of Christ's riches are needed most and how to present them in their best light.

This shows the nature and purpose of interfaith dialogue. Dialogue is neither a synonym nor a substitute for evangelism. Dialogue is a serious conversation in which we are prepared to listen and learn as well as to speak and teach. It is therefore an exercise in integrity. 'It is an activity in its own right,' Max Warren wrote. 'It is in its very essence an attempt at mutual "listening", listening in order to understand. Understanding is its reward.'[36] Warren knew what he was talking about, as he tells us in his autobiography:

> My earliest memory is of dancing firelight, and of my mother reading to me. I am looking into the flames and listening. I must have been three or four years old . . . Long before I could read I was learning to listen, perhaps the most valuable lesson I ever learnt . . . What is more, reading has always been for me a form of listening. Books have always been 'persons' to me, not just the person of the author so much as the book itself talking, while I listened.[37]

Second, there is the pain of the poor and the hungry, the dispossessed and the oppressed. Many of us have only relatively recently woken up to the obligation which Scripture has always laid on the people of God to care about social justice. We should be listening more attentively to the cries and sighs of those who are suffering. Here's a Bible verse which we have neglected, and which on that account we should perhaps underline. It contains a solemn word from God to those of his people who lack a social conscience. It is Proverbs 21:13: 'Whoever shuts their ears to the cry of the poor will also cry out and not be answered.'

To turn a deaf ear to somebody is a signal mark of disrespect. If we refuse to listen to someone, we are saying that we do not consider that person worth listening to. But there is only one person to whom we should refuse to listen on the grounds that he is not worth hearing and that is the devil, together with his emissaries. It is the essence of wisdom to be a discerning, discriminating listener and to choose carefully to whom we listen. Failure to do this was the folly of our first parents in the Garden of Eden. Instead of listening to the truth of God, they gave credence to the lies of Satan. And we are often crazy enough to copy them!

But we should not listen to the devil's talk, whether it be lies or propaganda, slander or gossip, filth or insults. 'The prudent overlook an insult.'[38] The same applies to anonymous letters or online comments. It is possible to be very upset by them, since they are usually rude. But why should we take seriously the criticisms of someone who lacks the courage to disclose their identity? Joseph Parker, a London minister in the nineteenth century, was climbing into his tall pulpit one Sunday morning when a woman in the gallery threw a piece of paper at him. Picking it up, he found that it contained a single word: 'Fool!' Dr Parker commented, 'I have received many anonymous letters in my life. Previously they have been a text without a signature. Today for the first time I have received a signature without a text!'

If we resolutely refuse to listen to anything that is untrue, unfair, unkind or impure, we should at the same time listen carefully to instruction and advice, criticism, reproof and correction, together with other people's views, concerns, problems and troubles. For, as has been well said, 'God has given us two ears, but only one mouth, so he evidently intends us to listen twice as much as we talk.'

To take time to listen to God and to our fellow human beings begins as a mark of courtesy and respect, continues as the means to mutual understanding and deepening relationships, and above all is an authentic token of Christian humility and love. So, 'everyone should be quick to listen, slow to speak and slow to become angry'.

Reflection questions from Tim Chester

1 Stott says, 'God speaks through what he has spoken.' What difference will it make when we view the Bible as the means through which God speaks today, as well as the record of what he spoke in the past?

2 Think of your home and workplace. Is there a relationship in which you need to listen more and speak less?

3 Think of an issue on which you disagree with another Christian. What lies behind what they are saying? What are they anxious to safeguard? What is the common ground you share?

4 Think of an individual or group you are trying to reach for Christ. What could you do to understand more deeply their thoughts, feelings and objections to the gospel?

5 'Whoever shuts their ears to the cry of the poor will also cry out and not be answered.'[39] What does it mean for you to *open* your ears to the poor?

6 Do you prefer to talk or to listen? What does this say about your attitude to God? To other people? What is the link between listening and loving?

2

Mind and emotions

Christian discipleship involves the whole of our personality. We are to love the Lord our God with all our heart, soul, mind and strength.[1] Our mind is to be renewed,[2] our emotions purified,[3] our conscience kept clear[4] and our will surrendered to God.[5] Discipleship entails all that we know of ourselves being committed to all that we know of God. Yet, of the various elements that go to make up our humanity, it is our mind and our emotions which the biblical writers treat most fully. So we will consider each separately, and then the two in relation to each other.

The mind

The story is told of two women who were having a chat in their local supermarket. One said to the other, 'What's the matter with you? You look so worried.'

'I am,' responded her friend. 'I keep thinking about the situation in the world.'

'Well,' said the first, 'you want to take things more philosophically, and stop thinking!'

It is a rather delicious idea that the way to become more philosophical is to do less thinking. Yet those two women were reflecting the modern anti-intellectual mood, which has given birth to the ugly twins of mindlessness and meaninglessness.

Against this trend we need to set the instruction of the apostle Paul: 'Brothers and sisters, stop thinking like children. In regard to evil be infants, but in your thinking be adults.'[6] He begins with the very words used by one of the women in the supermarket, 'stop

23

thinking'. But he continues, 'like children'. True, Jesus told us to become like children, but he did not mean that we are to copy children in everything. Similarly, Paul urges us to be children, indeed 'infants' or 'babies', in evil (the less sophisticated we are in relation to evil, the better). But in our thinking we are to grow up, to become mature. The revelation of the whole Bible lies behind Paul's appeal.

First, a responsible use of our minds *glorifies our Creator*. For he is (among other things) a rational God, who made us in his own image as rational beings. He has given us both in nature and in Scripture a rational revelation. And he expects us to use our minds to explore what he has revealed. All scientific research is based on the convictions that

- the universe is an intelligible, even meaningful, system;
- there is a fundamental correspondence between the mind of the investigator and the data being investigated; and
- this correspondence is rationality.

As a result, 'a scientist faced with an apparent irrationality does not accept it as final . . . He goes on struggling to find some rational way in which the facts can be related to each other . . . Without that passionate faith in the ultimate rationality of the world, science would falter, stagnate and die.'[7] It is therefore no accident that the pioneers of the scientific revolution were Christians. They believed that the rational God had stamped his rationality both upon the world and upon them. In this way all scientists, whether they know it or not, are 'thinking God's thoughts after him', as the seventeenth-century German astronomer Johannes Kepler put it.

Conscientious students of the Bible are also 'thinking God's thoughts after him'. For God has given us in Scripture an even clearer and fuller revelation of himself. He has 'spoken', communicating his thoughts in words. In particular, he has disclosed his love for sinners like us, and his plan to save us through Jesus Christ.

If God, then, has made us rational persons, how can we deny this essential feature of our creation? If he has taken the trouble to reveal himself, shall we neglect his revelation? No, the proper use of our minds is neither to abdicate our responsibility and go to sleep, nor to proclaim the autonomy of human reason (as the leaders of the Enlightenment did). We are not to stand in judgment on the data of divine revelation, but to sit in humility under them, to study, interpret, synthesize and apply them. Only in this way can we glorify our Creator.

Second, a responsible use of our minds *enriches our Christian life*. I am not now thinking of education, culture and art, which enhance the quality of human life, but specifically of our discipleship. We cannot be true disciples if we stifle our minds. 'Looking back over my experience as a pastor for some thirty-four years,' wrote Martyn Lloyd-Jones, 'I can testify without the slightest hesitation that the people I have found most frequently in trouble in their spiritual experience have been those who have lacked understanding. You cannot divorce these things. You will go wrong in the realms of practical living and experience if you have not a true understanding.'[8]

Let me illustrate this in relation to faith. It is amazing how many people suppose that faith and reason are incompatible. But they are never set against each other in Scripture. Faith and sight are contrasted,[9] but not faith and reason. For faith according to Scripture is neither credulity, nor superstition, nor 'an illogical belief in the occurrence of the improbable'.[10] Instead, faith is a quiet, thoughtful trust in the God who is known to be trustworthy. Consider Isaiah 26:3–4:

You will keep in perfect peace
   those whose minds are steadfast,
   because they trust in you.
Trust in the Lord for ever,
   for the Lord, the Lord himself, is the Rock eternal.

In these verses to trust in God and to set our minds steadfastly on him are synonyms. What makes trust in him rational is that he is an immovable rock, and the reward of faith is peace. It is only by reflecting on the changelessness of God that our faith grows. And the more we perceive how steadfast he is, the more steadfast our faith becomes.

Or take our need of divine guidance. Many people regard it as an alternative to human thought, even a convenient device to save them the bother of thinking. They expect God to flash into their minds answers to their questions and solutions to their problems, in a way that bypasses their minds. And of course God is free to do this; perhaps occasionally he does. But God's normal way of guiding us is rational, not irrational, using the very thought processes which he has created in us.

Psalm 32 makes this clear. Verse 8 contains a marvellous threefold promise of divine guidance, in which God says, 'I will instruct you and teach you in the way you should go; I will counsel you and watch over you' ('counsel you with my eye upon you', RSV). But *how* will God fulfil his promise? Verse 9 continues: 'Do not be like the horse or the mule, which have no understanding but must be controlled by bit and bridle or they will not come to you.' If we put together the promise and the prohibition, what God is saying to us is this: 'I promise that I will guide you, and show you the way to go. But do not expect me to guide you in the way people guide horses and mules (namely by force, rather than through intelligence). Why? Because you are neither a horse nor a mule. They lack "understanding", but you don't. Indeed, I myself have given you the precious gift of understanding. Use it! Then I will guide you *through* your minds.'

Third, a responsible use of our minds *strengthens our evangelistic witness.* So much modern evangelism is an appeal to the emotions and the will, without any comparable recognition of the mind. But our evangelistic appeal should never ask people to close or suspend their minds. The gospel requires us to humble our minds, but also to open them to God's truth.

We see this concern for the mind in the practice of the apostles. Paul tells the Corinthian church that he had renounced the wisdom of the world and the rhetoric of the Greeks,[11] but he did not renounce doctrinal content in his preaching, nor the use of arguments. In Corinth itself, Luke describes him as 'reasoning' with people and trying to 'persuade' them,[12] while in Ephesus he lectured and debated daily in a secular lecture hall for two years.[13] It is true that his confidence was in the Holy Spirit. But, being the Spirit of truth, the Holy Spirit brings people to faith in Christ because of the evidence, and not in spite of it. There is an urgent need in our day to include apologetics in our evangelism, that is, to defend the gospel as well as to proclaim it. In all our evangelism we need to be able to declare, as Paul did to Festus, 'What I am saying is true and reasonable.'[14] In addition, God is surely calling some people in our generation, as he has done in the past, to dedicate their God-given intellect to the task of 'defending and confirming the gospel'.[15]

So we need to repent of the cult of mindlessness, and any residual anti-intellectualism or intellectual laziness of which we may be guilty. These things are negative, confining and destructive. They insult God, impoverish his people and weaken our testimony. A responsible use of our minds, on the other hand, glorifies God, enriches his people and strengthens our witness in the world.

Two qualifications are needed, however, because there are two dangerous 'isms' which, if we are not on our guard, might result from this emphasis on the mind, namely elitism and intellectualism. Elitism would limit Christian thinking to a small minority of university-educated people. It would give the impression that only a select, even exclusive, bunch of eggheads are capable of using their minds. We must set ourselves fiercely against this bizarre notion. It is true that Christians have been the pioneers of education, and want everybody to have the best possible education to develop their maximum potential. But formal education is not indispensable for developing Christian thinking. For *all* human beings are created rational in God's image and are able to learn how to think. I once addressed a group of clergy in Liverpool and said something about the need to use our God-given minds. As soon as I had finished, somebody objected that I was limiting Christianity to intellectuals and excluding the working classes among whom he worked. I did not need to reply. For immediately several inner-city workers were on their feet, flushed with anger. 'You're insulting the working classes,' they said to the first speaker. 'They may not have had as much formal education as you, but they're just as intelligent and just as able to think.' Our task, then, is to encourage all God's people to think, and not merely to develop an intellectual elite.

The second danger is intellectualism, the encouragement of a Christianity that is too cerebral, and not visceral enough – all brain with no gut. But to urge people to use their minds does not mean urging them to suppress their feelings. I often say to our students at the London Institute for Contemporary Christianity that we are not in the business of 'breeding tadpoles'. A tadpole is a little creature with a huge head and nothing much else besides. Certainly there are some Christian tadpoles around. Their heads are bulging with sound theology, but that is all there is to them. No, we are concerned to help people develop not only a Christian mind, but also a Christian heart, a Christian spirit, a Christian conscience and a Christian will, in fact to become whole Christian persons, thoroughly integrated under the lordship of Christ. This will include our emotions.

Chaim Potok's book *The Chosen*[16] and the film based on it illustrate this well. He tells the story of two Jewish youths who were brought up in Brooklyn, New York, during and after the Second World War. Danny Saunders' father was a strict Hasidic rabbi, while Ruevan Malter's father was a writer in the liberal Jewish tradition. In the boys' friendship these two traditions came into conflict. Throughout most of the book Rabbi Saunders astonishes us because, although he is a very human person, he never talks to Danny except when he is teaching him out of the Talmud. Instead, he maintains between them a 'weird silence'.[17] Not until near the end is the mystery explained. Rabbi Saunders says that God had blessed him with a brilliant son, 'a boy with a mind like a jewel'. When Danny was only four years old, his father saw him reading a book and was frightened because he 'swallowed' it. The book described the sufferings of a poor Jew, yet Danny had enjoyed it! 'There was no soul in my four-year-old Daniel, there was only his mind. He was a mind in a body without a soul.'[18] So the rabbi cried to God, 'What have you done to me? A mind like this I need for a son? A *heart* I need for a son, a *soul* I need for a son, compassion . . . righteousness, mercy, strength to suffer and carry pain. *That* I want from my son, not a mind without a soul!'[19] So Rabbi Saunders followed an ancient Hasidic tradition and brought the boy up in silence, for then 'in the silence between us he began to hear the world crying'.[20] In the final scene of reconciliation between father and son, the rabbi says that Danny had to learn 'through the wisdom and the pain of silence that a mind without a heart is nothing'.

The emotions

My readers will probably not suspect me of being an emotional person. For I am one of those cold fish called an Englishman, descended from hard Norsemen and blunt Anglo-Saxons, with no spark of Celtic or Latin fire in my blood. With that ancestry, I am supposed to be shy, reserved and even a bit repressed. Moreover, I was brought up in an elite English school on the philosophy of the 'stiff upper lip'. Since a trembling of the upper lip is the first visible sign of emotion, we were taught to stiffen it. I was taught the 'manly' virtues of courage, fortitude and self-discipline. Should I ever feel any emotion, I learned on no account to show it. Weeping was strictly for women and children only, not for men.

But then I was introduced to Jesus Christ. I learned to my astonishment that God, whose 'impassibility' I thought meant that he was incapable of emotion, speaks (though in human terms) of his burning anger and vulnerable love.[21] I discovered too that Jesus of Nazareth, the perfect human being, was no tight-lipped, unemotional ascetic. On the contrary, I read that he turned on hypocrites with anger, looked on a rich young ruler and loved him, could both rejoice in spirit and sweat drops of blood in spiritual agony, was constantly moved with compassion, and even burst into tears twice in public.

From all this evidence it is plain that our emotions are not to be suppressed, since they have an essential place in our humanness and therefore in our Christian discipleship.

First, there is a place for emotion in *spiritual experience*. The Holy Spirit is the Spirit of truth, as we have seen. But his ministry is not limited to illuminating our minds and teaching us about Christ. He also pours God's love into our hearts.[22] He bears witness with our spirit that we are God's children, for he causes us to say '*Abba*, Father'[23] and to exclaim with gratitude, 'See what great love the Father has lavished on us, that we should be called children of God!'[24] In addition, although we have not yet seen Christ, nevertheless already we love him and trust him, and so 'are filled with an inexpressible and glorious joy'.[25]

There are, of course, many varieties of spiritual experience, and we must not try to stereotype them. Nor should we insist everybody has exactly the same experience. Nevertheless, all Christian people, at least from time to time, have feelings both of profound sorrow and of profound joy. On the one hand, we 'groan inwardly', in solidarity with the fallen creation, burdened with our own fallenness and longing for our final redemption.[26] On the other, we rejoice in the Lord, overwhelmed with gratitude for the great love with which he has loved us.

Second, there is a place for emotion in *public worship*. We are told in Hebrews 12:22–24 that when we assemble for worship, we do not just 'come to church', that is, to a building. For already we 'have come to Mount Zion, to the city of the living God, the heavenly Jerusalem'.

We 'have come to thousands upon thousands of angels in joyful assembly, to the church of the firstborn, whose names are written in heaven'. We 'have come to God, the judge of all, to the spirits of the righteous made perfect, to Jesus the mediator of a new covenant, and to the sprinkled blood that speaks a better word than the blood of Abel'. The recognition of this cosmic dimension transforms worship. Perhaps only a handful of God's people will gather when you meet this Sunday, and perhaps there will not be much diversity among you. But remember, as the 1928 Prayer Book put it, that we have come together 'in the presence of Almighty God and of the whole company of heaven'. And in the communion service we join 'with angels and archangels, and with all the company of heaven' in praising God's glorious name. We are transported beyond ourselves into eternal, unseen reality. We are moved by the glories of which we speak and sing, and we bow down before God in humble and joyful worship.

Third, there is a place for emotion in *gospel preaching*. The apostle Paul used his mind, as we have seen. He believed in the truth of his message. He took time and trouble to defend, explain, argue and proclaim it in its fullness. But his unfolding of the whole plan of God was never cold or arid. On the contrary, he wrote that God 'has committed to us the message of reconciliation. We are therefore Christ's ambassadors, as though God were making his appeal through us. We implore you on Christ's behalf: be reconciled to God.'[27] Paul was not satisfied with a statement of the gospel; he also begged people to respond to it. To his systematic exposition he added an urgent personal appeal. And often, he tells us, his proclamation was accompanied by tears.[28]

Some preachers are impeccable in both doctrine and diction, but would never lean over the pulpit with tears in their eyes, imploring people to be reconciled to God. Others whip themselves up into a frenzy of excitement, begging for a decision, but never make a careful, cogent statement of the gospel. Why must we polarize? It is the combination of truth and tears, of mind and emotion, of reason and passion, of exposition and appeal, which makes the authentic preacher. For 'What is preaching?' asked Dr Lloyd-Jones, and went on to answer his own question. 'Logic on fire! Eloquent reason! Are these contradictions? Of course they are not. Reason concerning this Truth ought to be mightily eloquent ... Preaching is theology coming through a man who is on fire.'[29]

Fourth, there is a place for emotion in *social and pastoral ministry*. In this, as in all things, Jesus himself is our perfect model. See him at the graveside of Lazarus, face to face with the reality of death. According to Scripture, death is an alien intrusion into God's good world, and is no part of either his original or his ultimate purpose. The Bible calls death an 'enemy', in fact 'the last enemy to be destroyed'.[30] How, then, will Jesus react when confronted by this arch-enemy of God and of the human race? He reacted, surprisingly, with two violent emotions.

First, he was moved with anger, or indignation. In John 11:33 and 38 we are told that he 'groaned' (AV), 'sighed' (NEB) or 'was deeply moved' (RSV, NIV). The Greek verb *enebrimēsato* (verse 33) means that he 'snorted'; the word is used literally of horses and metaphorically of indignation.[31] C. K. Barrett in his commentary on John 11 writes, 'It is beyond question that *embrimasthai* implies anger.' B. B. Warfield went even further: 'What John tells us ... is that Jesus approached the grave of Lazarus in a state not of uncontrollable grief but of irrepressible anger.' Why? Because he saw 'the evil of death, its unnaturalness, its "violent tyranny" as Calvin phrases it'. He 'burns with rage against the oppressor of men ... Fury seizes upon him; his whole being is discomposed and perturbed ... It is death that is the object of his wrath, and behind death him who has the power of death, and whom he has come into the world to destroy.'[32]

Then we are told of a second emotional response of Jesus, namely sorrow and compassion. On seven separate occasions in the Gospels, Jesus was 'moved with compassion'. He feels compassion, for example, towards the hungry and leaderless crowds, the widow of Nain, leprosy sufferers and a blind beggar. And in John 11 we read that 'Jesus wept' (verse 35) – not now tears of anger in the face of death, but tears of sympathy for the bereaved sisters. Is it not beautiful to see Jesus, when confronted by death and bereavement, so deeply moved? He felt indignation in the face of death, and compassion towards its victims. First, he 'snorted' (verse 33) and then he 'wept' (verse 35).

Speaking personally, I long to see more Christian anger towards evil in the world, and more Christian compassion for its victims. Think of social injustice and political tyranny, of the callous killing of human foetuses in the womb as if they were no more than pieces of tissue, or the cynical wickedness of drug-pushers and porn-ographers who make their fortunes out of other people's weaknesses and at the cost of their ruin. Since these and many other evils are hated by God, should his people not react against them in anger? And what about the victims of evil – the poor, the hungry and the homeless, street kids abandoned by their parents, unborn children at risk in a selfish society, tortured prisoners of conscience, and the alienated and lost who have never heard the gospel? Where is our sense of outrage? Where is the compassion of Jesus, which will express itself in practical action for those who suffer?

I do not know how much Christian profession Bob Geldof makes, but his social conscience and drive put many of us Christians to shame. What happened, then, to transform the 'scruffy Irish pop singer' into 'St Bob', the cult hero who alerted the world to the famine holocaust in Africa? Watching the televised news report on famine in Ethiopia towards the end of 1984, he experienced what one might call a 'secular conversion'. The people he saw on his TV screen were 'so shrunken by starvation that they looked like beings from another planet'.[33] 'I felt disgusted, enraged and outraged,' he said, 'but more than all those, I felt deep shame.'[34] Out of this experi-ence came Band Aid and Live Aid and other initiatives, which raised many millions of pounds. What drove him? It was a combination of 'pity and disgust'.[35]

Mind and emotions

So far we have looked at our intellect and our emotions separately, and we have seen that both have an indispensable place in our Christian discipleship. We are to be neither such emotional Christians that we never think, nor such intellectual Christians that we never feel. No, God has made us human beings, and human beings are created both rational and emotional.

But how are our mind and our emotions to be related to one another? There are two particular relationships which Scripture emphasizes, and in which the mind exercises the primary role. They are also complementary, in that the first is negative, and the second positive.

First and negatively, *the mind controls the emotions*, or should do so. There have always been some who campaign for the unfettered expression of human emotions. Bacchus, for example, whom the Greeks identified with Dionysus, was worshipped in orgies of wine, dance and sex. Popular Freudianism, which has not entirely grasped what Freud meant by 'repression', has taught the peril of suppressing our emotions. And some forms of existentialism have added impetus to these ideas by urging us to find our authenticity in being and expressing ourselves.

But Christians cannot possibly follow this teaching and give free rein to our emotions. For our whole human being has been tainted and twisted by inherited sin, and that includes our emotions. They are ambiguous because we are ambiguous. Some are good, but others evil, and we have to learn to discriminate between them.

Take anger. The instruction 'In your anger do not sin'[36] recognizes that there are two different kinds of anger. There is righteous anger, such as God himself feels towards evil. And there is unrighteous anger (contaminated by pride, envy, malice, spite and revenge) which is one of the 'acts of the flesh'.[37] Consequently, when feelings of anger arise within us, it would be foolish to give vent to them uncritically. Instead, we should say to ourselves, 'Wait a minute! What is this anger that is beginning to burn inside me? Is it righteous anger or unrighteous? Is it anger against evil, or merely injured vanity?'

Or take love. What should we say to a married man who confesses that he has fallen in love with another woman, that he cannot help himself, that this is 'the real thing' and that he must divorce his wife? I think we would have to say, 'Wait a minute! You are not the helpless victim of your emotions. You have accepted a lifelong commitment to your wife. You should (and can) put this other woman out of your mind.'

In these two examples, the one of anger and the other of love, there is a recognition that both emotions can be tainted with self-centredness, and that we should never give in to either anger or love without first asking ourselves some searching questions. In both cases, the mind is meant to stand guard over the emotions.

Second and positively, *the mind stimulates the emotions.* It is when we reflect on the truth that our heart catches fire. Think of the Emmaus disciples on the afternoon of Easter Day. The risen Lord joined them on their walk and explained to them from the Scriptures how the Messiah had to suffer before entering his glory. Later, after he had left them, they said to each other, 'Were not our hearts burning within us while he talked with us on the road and opened the Scriptures to us?'[38] This inner burning of the heart is a profound emotional experience, but it was Jesus' biblical teaching which prompted it. Nothing sets the heart ablaze like fresh views of truth. As F. W. Faber put it, 'Deep theology is the best fuel of devotion; it readily catches fire, and once kindled it burns long.'[39]

Or consider Paul's well-known statement that 'Christ's love compels us'.[40] Literally, it 'hems us in' or 'leaves us no choice' (NEB), so that we must live our lives for him. But how does the love of

Christ constrain or move us? Is it that we are overwhelmed emotionally at the foot of the cross? Yes and no! Yes, in that we cannot contemplate the cross and not be moved by it. But no, if we suppose that our mind plays no part in the process. For what Paul writes is that 'Christ's love compels us, because we are convinced that . . .' It is through certain convictions that Christ's love tightens its grip on us. In brief, it is because we have received our lives from Christ crucified and risen that we realize we must live them for him. It is as we reflect upon this logic that the fires of love within us are fanned into flame.

One more example. In the area of social responsibility it is essential that we both think clearly and feel deeply. A cool analysis of injustice is necessary, so long as it leads to hot anger and action.

It is important, then, to keep our mind and our emotions together, allowing our mind both to control and to stimulate our emotions. I think it was Bishop Handley Moule at the end of the last century who gave this good advice: 'Beware equally of an undevotional theology (i.e. mind without heart) and of an untheological devotion (i.e. heart without mind).'

Reflection questions from Tim Chester

1 What impetus to science and scientific investigation does Christianity provide?
2 What is the link between reason and faith?
3 In which ways do you glorify God by using your mind?
4 There is a place for emotion in spiritual experience, public worship, gospel preaching (or personal evangelism), social and pastoral ministry. Is there an area in your life in which emotion is lacking?
5 Stott says the mind should control the emotions. Can you think of examples of the emotions controlling the mind? What were the causes and outcomes of this?

6 What's your biggest danger: undevotional theology (mind without heart) or untheological devotion (heart without mind)? How can you avoid this danger?

3

Guidance, vocation and ministry

If God has a purpose for the lives of his people, and if his purpose can be discovered, then nothing could be more important than for us to discern and do it. This was certainly the apostle Paul's expectation. 'We are God's workmanship,' he affirmed, 'created in Christ Jesus to do good works, which God prepared in advance for us to do.'[1] If, therefore, there are good works which God has designed for us, presumably from before we were born, we surely must find out what they are. No wonder Paul wrote later in the same letter, 'Do not be foolish, but understand what the Lord's will is.'[2]

In the companion letter to the Colossians Paul also prayed that God would 'fill [them] with the knowledge of his will through all spiritual wisdom and understanding'.[3] He told them Epaphras was 'always wrestling in prayer' for them, that they might 'stand firm in all the will of God, mature and fully assured'.[4]

Whenever we talk about discovering God's will for our lives, three words are almost always bound to crop up in the conversation: 'guidance', 'vocation' and 'ministry'. Each has a distinctive meaning. 'Guidance' implies that God is willing to direct us, 'vocation' that he calls us, and 'ministry' that he wants us to give our lives in service. What is common to all three concepts is that the initiative is God's. And each has both a general aspect (which applies equally to all of us) and a particular (which is different for each of us). This will become clearer as we go on.

Guidance

We sometimes say with a sigh, 'If only I had ten lives . . .' There is a myth that cats have nine, but we human beings have only one, and we cannot duplicate or replicate ourselves. Hence, our urgent need to discover God's will for the one and only life he has given us.

But before we are in a position to discover God's will, it is essential to draw a distinction between his 'general' will and his 'particular' will. God's general will is so called because it is his will for all his people in general. It is the same for all of us in all places and at all times. God's particular will is so called, however, because it is his will for particular people at particular places and times. His general will is that we should 'be conformed to the image of his Son'.[5] Christlikeness is God's will for all of us and does not vary from disciple to disciple. His particular will, on the other hand, concerns such questions as the choice of a life work and a life partner, as well as how we should spend our energies, time, money and holidays. These will be different for each of us. We need to keep this distinction between the 'general' and the 'particular' when we think about how we can discover God's will. His general will has been revealed in Scripture. Not that Scripture contains slick solutions to complex modern ethical problems, but it contains principles that can be applied to them. Generally speaking, it is correct to say that the will of God for the people of God is in the Word of God.

The particular will of God will not be found in Scripture, however. I cannot deny that occasionally God seems to have guided individuals through a specific verse wrenched out of its context. But I must add that he has done so only to accommodate to our weakness. For Scripture is not an anthology of unrelated texts, but a cumulative, historical revelation. We have no liberty to ignore its original meaning in order to make it speak to us. What the Bible does contain, however, is principles which are relevant to particular questions. Take marriage as an example. Scripture gives us general guidance

39

and settles some issues in advance. It tells us that marriage is God's good purpose for human beings and that singleness is the exception, not the rule. It tells us that one of his primary purposes in instituting marriage is companionship, so that this is an important quality to look for in a spouse. It tells us that a Christian can only marry a fellow-Christian, and that marriage (as a lifelong, loving, monogamous and heterosexual commitment) is the only God-ordained context for sexual intercourse. These general guidelines are clearly laid down in the Bible. But the Bible will not tell any individuals whether God is calling them to be married or to remain single, or (if they should marry) who their spouse ought to be.

How then are we meant to discover God's particular will, if he does not disclose it through Scripture? Since God is sovereign and free, I do not think we have the freedom to stereotype our answer as if one size fits all. But I have found that the following five short words are safe guides.

First, *yield*. The word is a familiar road sign in the United States, telling traffic to give way to other vehicles. In the same way, we are to give in to, or give way to, God's purpose. An unsurrendered will is the most serious of all obstacles to discovering God's will. If God does not reveal his truth to those who are unwilling to believe it, neither does he reveal his will to those unwilling to do it. No, 'He guides the humble in what is right and teaches them his way.'[6]

Second, *pray*. A vague surrender is not enough; sustained, expectant prayer is also necessary. 'Ask and it will be given to you,' Jesus taught. James added, 'You do not have, because you do not ask God.'[7] Our heavenly Father does not spoil his children. He does not disclose his will to us unless we really want to know it and express our desire in our prayers.

Third, *talk*. Although one of the strengths of Protestant Christianity is its insistence on 'the right of private judgment', we must not imagine this means we should make all our decisions alone. On the contrary, God has given us to each other in his family. So we need to be humble enough to talk to others, including our parents, in order to seek their counsel, for 'wisdom is found in those who take advice'.[8] Let our decisions be group decisions, taken responsibly in the rich fellowship in which God has put us.

Fourth, *think*. Although we must yield, pray and ask advice, ultimately we have to make up our own minds. As we saw in the last chapter, God balances his promises of guidance with his prohibition of behaviour like horses and mules which lack understanding.[9] We must not expect him to fulfil his promises to guide us either by using 'bit and bridle' (i.e. force) or by giving us irrational hunches. Instead, we should expect him to guide us through the minds he has given us, as we carefully weigh up the pros and cons.

Fifth, *wait*. It is a mistake to be in a hurry or grow impatient with God. It took him about 2,000 years to fulfil his promise to Abraham in the birth of Christ. It took him eighty years to prepare Moses for his life work. It takes him about twenty-five years to make a mature human being. So, then, if we *have* to make a decision by a certain deadline, we must make it. But if not, and the way forward is still uncertain, it is wiser to wait. I think God says to us what he said to Joseph and Mary when sending them into Egypt with the child Jesus: 'Stay there until I tell you.'[10] In my experience, more mistakes are made by precipitous action than by procrastination.

Vocation

'Vocation' is one of many biblical words which over the years has changed its meaning and become devalued. In popular usage it refers to our work or career. 'What's your vocation?' is a rather grandiose way of asking somebody what his or her job is, and 'vocational training' means training for a particular trade. In biblical usage, however, 'vocation' has a much broader and nobler connotation. Its emphasis is not on the human (what *we* do) but on the divine (what *God* has called us to do). 'Vocation' comes from the Latin word for 'calling'.

In the New Testament the Greek verb to 'call' occurs about 150 times, and in most cases it refers to God calling human beings. In the Old Testament God called Moses, Samuel and the prophets; in the New Testament Jesus called the Twelve and later Saul of Tarsus. Today, although we are neither prophets nor apostles, he still calls us into his service. It is a wonderful fact that God cares about us enough to call us personally and individually. In consequence, God is 'he who called you',[11] and we are those who have been 'called according to his purpose'.[12]

The question we need to address is this: what, according to Scripture, does God call us to? What is our divine vocation? To answer this question we have to make a similar distinction to the one we made with 'guidance', namely between our 'general' calling and our particular 'callings'. Our general calling is that of all God's people, and is therefore the same. Our particular calling is that of each of us, and is therefore different. We all share in the same general call of God; we have each received a different particular call from God.

God's *general call* to us is not so much to do something (a job) as to be something (a person). Although he does call us to different tasks, as we shall shortly see, he first calls us to something even more significant, namely to be a disciple of Jesus Christ, to live a new life in his new society and in the world. So if somebody asks us, 'What is your calling?', our first and correct answer should be: 'I am called to belong to Jesus Christ.'[13] In fact, we are called to embrace and enjoy all the blessings which God has locked up in Jesus Christ: 'to this you were called so that you may inherit a blessing.'[14] What, then, is this blessing? It has many facets.

First, we are called to *fellowship with Jesus Christ*. This is basic. His invitation is still 'Come to me' and 'Follow me'. For 'God . . . has called you into fellowship with his Son, Jesus Christ our Lord'.[15] Just as Christ called the Twelve to be 'with him',[16] so he calls us to know him and to enjoy his fellowship. Eternal life is to know God and his

Christi,[17] and nothing can take the place of this fundamental relationship with him.

Second, we are called to *freedom*. 'You, my brothers and sisters,' Paul wrote to the Galatians, 'were called to be free.'[18] The kind of freedom to which the apostle was alluding here is freedom from the condemnation of the law through God's forgiveness and acceptance in Christ. It is freedom from guilt and from a guilty conscience, the freedom of access to God as his adopted sons and daughters. It is not, however, freedom to sin or freedom from social responsibilities. On the contrary, Paul goes on, 'But do not use your freedom to indulge the flesh; rather, serve one another [literally, "be slaves to one another"] in love.' It is the paradox we have already seen that it is only through serving that we become free.

Third, we are called to *peace*. 'Let the peace of Christ rule in your hearts, since as members of one body you were called to peace.'[19] The reference to the 'one body' gives us the clue to Paul's meaning. He is here referring not to peace of mind, heart or conscience, but to the peace (*shalom*) of reconciliation with each other in the kingdom community of Christ. Our calling is to belong not only to Christ, but also to the people of Christ.

Fourth, we are called to *holiness*,[20] or 'called to be saints'.[21] Since God himself is holy, he calls us to be holy too.[22] Unfortunately, 'holiness' suggests to many a false image of pious detachment, people with colourless lives and vacant stares, who have contracted out of life. But true holiness is a Christlikeness which is lived out in the real world.

Fifth, we are called to *witness*. 'But you are . . . God's special possession, that you may declare the praises of him who called you out of darkness into his wonderful light.'[23] Peter is contrasting what we once were with what we now are. We were in darkness, but now we are in light. We were not a people, but now we are God's people. We had not received mercy, but now we have. The logical deduction is that we cannot possibly keep these blessings to ourselves.

Having been called into God's light, we are inevitably called to let our light shine.

Sixth, we are called to *suffering*. 'If you suffer for doing good and you endure it, this is commendable before God. To this you were called.'[24] Peter was writing when Nero's hostility to Christians was growing and the storm clouds of persecution were gathering ominously on the horizon. At any moment the storm might break. How then should Christians react if they suffered unjustly? Peter's answer was straightforward. They were called to follow Christ's example of non-retaliation. It comes as a shock to many people that unjust suffering is an unavoidable part of the Christian calling. But Jesus himself warned us of it. 'If the world hates you, keep in mind that it hated me first . . . If they persecuted me, they will persecute you also.'[25]

Seventh, we are called to *glory*. The Christian calling is a 'heavenly calling'.[26] 'The God of all grace, who called you to his eternal glory in Christ, after you have suffered a little while, will himself . . . make you strong, firm and steadfast.'[27] Suffering and glory are constantly linked together in the New Testament. It was through suffering that Jesus entered his glory, and it will be the same for us. If we share in Christ's suffering, we will also share in his glory.[28] Thus, the call of God is not for this life only; it is also to spend eternity with him in the new universe.

Here, then, is God's sevenfold, general calling. He calls all of us to Christ, freedom, peace, holiness, witness, suffering and glory. More simply, it is a call to belong to Christ in time and eternity, to love one another in the peace of his new community, and to serve, witness and suffer in the world. This is the fundamental meaning of 'Christian vocation'. It is the same for all of us, and we are exhorted to live a life that is worthy of it.[29]

If our general call (which is the same for us all) is to be free and holy and Christlike, our *particular calling* (which is different for each of us) relates to the individual details of our lives. Consider the teaching of Paul: 'Each person should remain in the situation [literally, "the calling"] they were in when God called them.'[30] We note at once the two senses in which the apostle uses the notion of 'calling'. The words 'when God called them' refer to a person's conversion when God's general call is heard and obeyed. 'The situation' ('calling') which the person was 'in', on the other hand, is a reference to the particular calling at the time of his or her conversion. This situation is regarded as something God has 'called' us to and something God has 'assigned' to us.[31] And the general principle the apostle lays down, repeating it three times,[32] is that we should 'remain' in it. He gives three examples – our domestic situation (married or single), our cultural situation (Jewish or Gentile) and our social situation (slaves or free). In order to understand Paul's teaching, we need to grasp the background and context. It appears that the Corinthian converts found life in Christ so exciting and new ('a new creation'),[33] and so radically different from their unregenerate state, that they imagined that nothing belonging to the old life could be retained; everything had to be rejected.

Take the example of marriage. Now that they belonged to Christ, they seem to have been asking, how could a pre-conversion contractual obligation still be valid post-conversion? Would not such a relationship be 'unclean'?[34] Paul answers, 'No.' Why not? Because God's providence embraced both their pre- and their post-conversion lives. Their marriage, though entered into before they became Christians, was a part of the 'calling' they were in when God called them. So they were not free to reject it. Transform it by God's grace – yes; reject it – no.

We have to be very cautious in applying this teaching to ourselves. Paul is laying down a general rule, not an absolute one. For example, he himself had not remained a Pharisee when called to be an apostle of Christ. Similarly, the Twelve had given up their fishing and their tax-collecting when called to become apostles. And Paul says here that if a slave can gain his freedom he should do so.[35] We too need to be open to the possibility that God is calling us to something different. What Paul was opposing was thoughtless and reckless actions, change for change's sake, and especially the notion that nothing before conversion and nothing outside religion has any value to God.

From Scripture we turn to history, and the teaching of the Reformers and the Puritans. The Reformers insisted that every Christian has a divine 'calling'. They were reacting against the teaching of medieval Catholicism which said bishops, priests, monks and nuns had a superior calling because it was a 'religious' calling. The Reformers rejected this as both 'clericalism' (separating clergy from laity) and 'dualism' (separating 'sacred' activities like prayer from 'secular' ones like running a home or earning a living). They affirmed that God is interested in the whole of life. To be a farmer, craftsperson, magistrate or housewife was just as much a divine calling as to be a 'priest' or 'pastor'. Martin Luther said,

> Those who are now called 'spiritual', that is, priests, bishops or popes, are neither different from other Christians nor superior to them, except that they are charged with the administration of the word of God and the sacraments, which is their work and office.

But 'tailors, cobblers, stonemasons, carpenters, cooks, innkeepers, farmers and all the temporal craftsmen' have also been 'consecrated' like priests, each to 'the work and office of his trade'.

> Further, everyone must benefit and serve every other by means of his own work or office, so that in this way many kinds of work may be done for the bodily and spiritual welfare of the community, just as all the members of the body serve one another (1 Corinthians 12:14–26).[36]

Again, 'Serving God is not tied to one or two works, nor is it confined to one or two callings, but it is distributed over all works and all callings.'[37] 'But what I want to do is to keep a distinction between the callings and offices, so that everyone can see to what God has called him and fulfil the duties of his office faithfully and sincerely in the service of God.'[38]

Calvin's teaching was similar:

> The Lord bids each one of us in all life's actions to look to his calling . . . Therefore, lest through our stupidity and rashness everything be turned topsy-turvy, he has appointed duties for every man in his particular way of life. And that no one may thoughtlessly transgress his limits, he has named these various kinds of living 'callings'. Therefore each individual has his own kind of living assigned to him by the Lord as a sort of sentry post so that he may not heedlessly wander about throughout life . . . From this will arise also a singular consolation: that no task will be so sordid and base, provided you obey your calling in it, that it will not shine and be reckoned very precious in God's sight.[39]

The Puritans developed this theme further. William Perkins, for example, who had a very influential ministry in Cambridge, wrote *A Treatise of the Vocations or Callings of Men* (published in 1603). Here is a sample of his argument:

> The action of a shepherd in keeping sheep . . . is as good a work before God as is the action of a judge in giving sentence, or of a magistrate in ruling, or a minister in preaching. Thus then we see there is good reason why we would search how every man is rightly to use his particular calling.[40]

A century later, and on the other side of the Atlantic, Cotton Mather, the Harvard Puritan, wrote *A Christian at His Calling* (1701).

In it he taught that every Christian has two callings – 'a general calling' ('to serve the Lord Jesus Christ') and 'a personal calling' ('a particular employment by which his usefulness in his neighbourhood is distinguished').[41] These two callings should be pursued in balance. For 'a Christian at his two callings is a man in a boat rowing for heaven . . . If he mind but one of his callings, be it which it will, he pulls the oar but on one side of the boat, and will make but a poor dispatch to the shore of eternal blessedness.'[42]

It would be easy to criticize this kind of teaching. The Reformers and the Puritans were people of their age and culture, as we are of ours. They held a static, medieval view of society. In their reaction against the revolutionary overtones of some Anabaptist teaching, they tended to be too resistant to change. Sometimes they got close to the embarrassing verse in the hymn 'All Things Bright and Beautiful':

> The rich man in his castle,
>   The poor man at his gate,
> God made them, high or lowly,
>   And ordered their estate.

We certainly should not use the biblical teaching about 'callings' to resist social change.

Paul in the first century, the Reformers in the sixteenth and the Puritans in the seventeenth all seem rather remote from us. So what is the underlying principle, which Paul taught and the Reformers and Puritans recovered, and which we need to hold on to today? I think it is this. The whole of our lives belong to God and are part of his calling, both before conversion and outside religion. We must not imagine that God first became interested in us when we were converted, or that now he is interested only in the religious bit of our lives.

Consider our life before conversion. What was the calling in which we were when God called us? If at the time of our conversion we were looking after elderly relatives, we should not abandon them now. If we were students, we are not free to give up our studies and drop out of university. If we had entered into a contract with somebody, we have no right to break it. If we were musical, artistic, athletic or intelligent when God called us, we must not now disown these good things which a good Creator gave us. For these things were not accidental aspects of our life. They were part of God's providence to which he had called us and which he had assigned to us. God's sovereignty extends over both halves of our life. He did not begin to work in and for us at our conversion. He was at work in us even before our birth in our genetic inheritance, and then later in our temperament, personality, education and skills. And what God made us and gave us before we became Christians, he redeems, sanctifies and transforms afterwards. There is a vital continuity between our pre- and post-conversion life. For, although we are a new person in Christ, we are still the same person we were by creation, whom Christ has made new.

Now consider our life outside religion. The God many of us worship is altogether too religious. We seem to imagine that he is interested only in religious books and buildings and services. But no, he is interested in *us*, in our home, family and friends, in our work and hobbies, in our citizenship and community. So God's sovereignty extends over *both* halves and over *all* sections of our lives. We must not marginalize God, or try to squeeze him out of the non-religious section of our lives. We must remember that our vocation (i.e. God's calling) includes these things. It is in these that we are to serve and glorify God.

Ministry

If we are concerned to discover where God is leading us (guidance) and to what he is calling us (vocation), we may be sure that this will be connected to how best we may serve him (ministry). Moreover, as with the words 'guidance' and 'vocation', so with the word 'ministry', we need to distinguish between a broader and a narrower meaning, between a general and a particular application.

Here are three affirmations about ministry.

First, *all Christians without exception are called to ministry*. Indeed, we are to give our lives in ministry. Ministry is the privilege not of a small elite, but of all the disciples of Jesus. You will have noticed that I did not say that all Christians are called to *the* ministry, but to ministry, *diakonia*, service. We do a great disservice to the Christian cause whenever we refer to being a pastor as being in 'the ministry'. For we give the impression that pastoral ministry is the only ministry there is, much as medieval churchmen regarded the priesthood as the only (or at least the most 'spiritual') vocation there is. Whenever somebody says in my presence that 'so-and-so is going into the ministry', I always ask innocently, 'Oh really? Which ministry do you mean?' If they reply, as they often do, 'The pastoral ministry', then I come back with the gentle complaint, 'Then why didn't you say so?!' The fact is that the word 'ministry' is a generic term which lacks specificity until we add an adjective.

I come back to my first proposition that all Christians without exception are called to ministry. How can I make such a dogmatic statement? Because of Jesus Christ. His lordship over us has a vocational dimension. Since he is 'the servant' par excellence, who gave himself without reserve to the service of God and human beings, it would be impossible to be his disciple without seeking to follow his example of service. He preached the kingdom, healed the sick, fed the hungry, befriended the friendless, championed the oppressed, comforted the bereaved, sought the lost and washed his apostles' feet. No task was too demanding, and no ministry too menial, for him to undertake. He lived his life and died his death in complete self-forgetful service. Shall we not imitate him? The world measures greatness by success; Jesus measures it by service.

Second, *there is a wide variety of Christian ministries.* This is because 'ministry' means 'service', and there are many different ways in which we can serve God and people. Acts 6:1–4 provides a firm biblical base for this conviction. An ethnic or cultural squabble was tearing the Jerusalem church apart. The 'Grecian Jews' were complaining against the 'Hebraic Jews' because they thought their widows were being discriminated against in the daily distribution of food. The apostles had become embroiled in this quarrel, and it was occupying a great deal of their time, and threatening to distract them from the preaching and teaching role to which Jesus had commissioned them. So they wisely called a church meeting and said, 'It would not be right for us to neglect the ministry of the word of God in order to wait on [*diakonein*] tables.' The church was then asked to choose seven men for that responsibility. This would allow the apostles to 'give our attention to prayer and the ministry [*diakonia*] of the word'.

It is essential to note that both distributing food and teaching the Word were referred to as ministry (*diakonia*). Both were Christian ministry, could be full-time Christian ministry, and required Spirit-filled people to perform them. The only difference between them was that one was pastoral ministry, and the other social. It was not that one was 'ministry' and the other not; nor that one was spiritual and the other secular; nor that one was superior and the other inferior. It was simply that Christ had called the Twelve to the ministry of the Word and the Seven to the ministry of tables.

I was brought up as a young Christian to think of different vocations or ministries as forming a hierarchy or pyramid. Perched precariously at the top of the pyramid were the cross-cultural missionaries. They were our heroes. I was taught that if I was really out and out for Christ, then I would undoubtedly join their ranks overseas. If I was not as keen as that, I would stay at home and be a pastor. If I did not aspire even to that, I would probably become a doctor or a teacher. But if I were to go into business, politics or the media, then I would not be far from backsliding! Please do not misunderstand me. It is a wonderful privilege to be a missionary or a pastor, *if God calls us to it*. But it is equally wonderful to be a Christian lawyer, industrialist, politician, manager, social worker, television script-writer, journalist or home-maker, *if God calls us to it*. According to Romans 13:4, an official of the state (whether legislator, magistrate or police officer) is just as much a 'minister of God' (*diakonos theou*) as a pastor. It is the hierarchy we have to reject; the pyramid we have to demolish.

There is still, of course, an urgent need for missionaries – people who are characterized above all by humility. We need missionaries with the humility to repent of cultural imperialism and identify with another culture, the humility to work under national church leadership, the humility to serve people's felt needs (social as well as evangelistic), and the humility to rely on the Holy Spirit as the chief communicator.[43] World evangelization remains at the top of the church's agenda. Pastors also are greatly needed to teach the Word of God.

At the same time, there is a crying need for Christians who see their daily work as their primary Christian ministry and who are determined to penetrate their secular environment for Christ.

Christians are needed in business and industry who see 'service to the public' as the first goal on their 'mission' statement, who make bold experiments in working relations, worker participation and profit-sharing, and who accept their responsibility to produce an annual 'social audit' alongside their annual financial audit.

Christian politicians are needed to identify the major injustices in their society, refuse to come to terms with them, and determine to secure legislative change, however long it takes. And Christian economists are needed to find ways of both creating and sharing wealth.

Christian film-makers are needed to produce not only overtly Christian or evangelistic films, but also wholesome films which indirectly commend Christian values, and so honour Christ.

More Christian doctors are needed who, in cooperation with moral theologians, face the contemporary challenges of medical ethics and develop ways of maintaining the uniquely Christian vision of the human person and the human family.

Dedicated Christian teachers are needed, in both Christian and secular schools, who count it a privilege to serve their students and help them develop their full God-given potential.

And more Christian social workers are needed who, in their concern for those with mental and physical disabilities, abused children, drug-abusers, AIDS victims and others, combine the latest medical treatment and social care with Christian love, believing prayer and church support.

Third, *the particular ministry to which Christ calls us is likely to be determined by our gifts.* The major factor determining our ministry focus will probably be what kind of person we are by God's creation and redemption. God is not a random creator; he has not given us natural gifts in order that they may be wasted. Nor is he a random redeemer, who has given us spiritual gifts to be wasted. Instead, he wants his gifts to be discerned, cultivated and exercised. He surely does not want us to be frustrated (because our gifts are lying idle), but rather fulfilled (because our gifts are being used).

It seems to me fully compatible with our Christian doctrines of creation and redemption that we should talk to ourselves somewhat as follows: 'I am a unique person. (That is not conceit. It is a fact. If every snowflake and every blade of grass is unique, how much more is every human being?) My uniqueness is due to my genetic make-up, my inherited personality and temperament, my parentage, upbringing and education, my talents, inclinations and interests, my new birth and spiritual gifts. By the grace of God I am who I am. How, then, can I, as the unique person God has made me, be *stretched* in the service of Christ and of people, so that nothing he has given me is wasted, and everything he has given me is used?'

There may be exceptions to this principle, but it appears to me to be the right question to ask oneself. And in trying to evaluate ourselves honestly in this way, with neither pride nor false modesty, our parents and friends who know us best are likely to help us most.

The three words we have been considering (guidance, vocation and ministry) all relate to God's will for our lives and how to discover it. As I conclude, let me anticipate two fears which my readers may be feeling, and try to relieve them.

First, there is no need to fear God's will on the assumption that it is bound to be difficult. Some Christians seem to imagine that the more disagreeable an option is, the more likely it is to be God's will! But God is not an ogre, bent on spoiling our lives. He is our Father, committed to our welfare and determined to give us only what is for our good. 'If you . . . though you are evil, know how to give good gifts to your children,' Jesus said, 'how much more will your Father in heaven give good gifts to those who ask him!'[44] We can be assured that God's will is 'good, pleasing and perfect'.[45]

Second, there is no need to fear that we shall never discover God's will. We have no reason to fret or worry, to work ourselves into a state of nervous tension, or spend sleepless nights of anxiety. Strangely enough, one of my earliest childhood memories, when I cannot have been more than six or seven, was of my mother coming into my bedroom daily to say goodnight. I plagued her with the constantly repeated, anguished question: 'Mummy, what am I going to be when I grow up?' She replied to the effect that I need not worry, since it would be shown me in due time. And now, more than sixty years later, with the benefit of hindsight, I know that she was right, and that all those childish worries were unnecessary. We have every reason to be confident that our Father's will is discoverable as well as good. He has ways and means of showing us what he wants us to do. The main condition is that we ourselves really want to discern his will, in order to do it.

Reflection questions from Tim Chester

1 How does Stott say the general will of God applies to marriage? How does it apply to work?

2 Do you agree that God has a specific will for our lives that we must discern? What biblical evidence supports your answer?

3 Think of a recent decision you faced. What helped you make your decision? Can you connect your decision-making process to Stott's model of yield, pray, talk, think and wait?

4 What is the link between our general calling and our specific calling? How should our general calling shape the way we fulfil our specific calling?

5 Talk of 'a calling' can sound somewhat static and outdated in an age in which people change jobs, employers and even careers several times during their working lives. How does what Stott describes as the 'underlying principle' of vocation suggest it might still be relevant?

6 What does it mean for you to see your work (whatever and wherever that may be) as ministry?

4

The first fruit of the Spirit

I invite you now to reflect on a biblical text that has come to mean much to me. Every day for perhaps twenty years I have quoted it to myself in my morning devotions, and prayed for its fulfilment in my life. When I am asked what my favourite text is, I usually give this one. It seems to me to contain truths which are of enormous importance to all the people of God. Here it is: 'But the fruit of the Spirit is love, joy, peace, forbearance, kindness, goodness, faithfulness, gentleness and self-control. Against such things there is no law.'[1]

From these two verses I think we may legitimately derive five affirmations about love.

Love, joy and peace

The first truth is that *love is the pre-eminent Christian grace*: 'the fruit of the Spirit is love'. True, Paul lists a cluster of nine qualities, which together he calls the Spirit's 'fruit', but love has pride of place. We hear much about the Holy Spirit nowadays (he is no longer the 'neglected' person of the Trinity), and many people are claiming spectacular manifestations of his power, but the first fruit of his indwelling presence is not power, but love.

What is the chief distinguishing mark of a Christian? What is the hallmark that authenticates people as the children of God? Different answers are given by different people.

Some reply that what distinguishes the genuine Christian is *truth*, orthodoxy, correct belief, loyalty to the doctrines of Scripture, the Catholic Creeds and the Reformation Confessions. Right! Truth is sacred. Sound doctrine is vital to the health of the church. We are summoned to 'fight the good fight of the faith',[2] to 'guard the deposit' of revealed religion,[3] to 'stand firm and hold fast to the teachings' of the apostles[4] and to 'contend for the faith that was once for all entrusted to God's holy people'.[5] We must never forget these solemn exhortations. Nevertheless, 'If I . . . can fathom all mysteries and all knowledge . . . but do not have love, I am nothing.'[6] Besides, 'knowledge puffs up, but love builds up'.[7] So love is greater than knowledge.

Others insist that the hallmark of genuine disciples is *faith*. 'For we maintain that a person is justified by faith apart from the works of the law.'[8] As Martin Luther wrote, justification by faith is 'the principal article of all Christian doctrine' which 'maketh true Christians indeed'.[9] And Thomas Cranmer, the English Reformer and Archbishop, added the negative counterpart: 'This [doctrine] whosoever denieth is not to be counted for a true Christian man.'[10] Or to quote from a more modern evangelical statement, justification by faith is 'the heart and hub, the paradigm and essence, of the whole economy of God's saving grace'.[11] I agree. *Sola fide*, 'by faith alone', which was the watchword of the Reformation, must be our watchword too. Nevertheless, 'if I have a faith that can move mountains, but have not love, I am nothing'.[12] The great apostle of faith is clear that love is greater than faith.

A third group emphasizes *religious experience* as the hallmark of the Christian, often of a particular and vivid kind of experience which they believe must be reproduced in everybody. And this group also is to some extent correct. A first-hand personal relationship with God through Christ is essential. The internal witness of the Spirit is real. There is such a thing as 'unutterable and exalted joy',[13] and 'because of the surpassing greatness of knowing Christ Jesus my Lord', everything else is indeed a loss.[14] Nevertheless, 'if I speak in the tongues of men and of angels' and 'if I have the gift of prophecy' (claiming a direct communication from God), 'but do not have love, I am nothing'.[15] So love is greater than experience.

A fourth and final category of people, being of a practical bent, emphasize *service* as the distinguishing mark of the people of God, especially the service of the poor. Right again! Without good works faith is dead. Since Jesus was himself a champion of the poor, his disciples must be also. If we see people in need, and have the capacity to meet it, but do not take pity on them, how can we claim to have God's love in us?[16] Nevertheless, 'if I give away all I have, and if I deliver my body to be burned' (perhaps in a heroic gesture of sacrifice), 'but have not love, I gain nothing'.[17] So love is greater than service.

To sum up, knowledge is vital, faith indispensable, religious experience necessary and service essential, but Paul gives precedence to love. Love is the greatest thing in the world. For 'God is love'[18] in his innermost being. Father, Son and Spirit are eternally united to each other in self-giving love. So he who is love, and has set his love upon us, calls us to love him and others in return. 'We love because he first loved us.'[19] Love is the principal, the paramount, the pre-eminent, the distinguishing characteristic of the people of God. Nothing can dislodge or replace it. Love is supreme.

Second, *love brings joy and peace*. For 'the fruit of the Spirit is love, joy, peace'. The sequence is surely significant.

Human beings have always pursued joy and peace, though they have usually employed the more secular word 'happiness'. Thomas Jefferson, before becoming the third President of the United States, was so convinced that 'the pursuit of happiness' was an inalienable human right that he wrote it into the Declaration of Independence and called it a 'self-evident truth'.

But Christians feel obliged to add that those who pursue happiness never find it. Joy and peace are extremely elusive blessings. Even as we reach out a hand to grasp hold of happiness, we find it vanishing into thin air. For joy and peace are not suitable goals to pursue; they are by-products of love. God gives them to us, not when we pursue *them*, but when we pursue *him* and *others* in love.

It is urgent that we bear witness to this truth in the contemporary world, in which 'self-realization' is the trend and all the talk is of the importance of boosting a person's 'self-esteem'. In his perceptive book *Psychology as Religion*,[20] subtitled *The Cult of Self-Worship*, Dr Paul Vitz of New York University analysed the four principal 'self-theorists' of that decade – Erich Fromm (who argued that indifference to one's self is a vice, while self-affirmation is a virtue), Carl Rogers (whose 'client-centred' therapy aimed to help a client become an integrated, autonomous person through 'unconditional self-regard'), Abraham Maslow (who emphasized creative 'self-actualization') and Rollo May (who, influenced by existentialism, stressed decision and commitment as the means to becoming oneself). These four writers were all self-confessed secular humanists. They believed in human beings, not in God. They have had many popularizers, and their basic emphasis on self-esteem and self-actualization seems to have seeped into almost every segment of society. Dr David Wells comments that by the mid-1980s, '87.5% of what was published in the USA was catering to the interests and appetites of the self-movement'.[21]

It is true that there is a right and healthy kind of self-affirmation, which balances the self-denial to which Jesus called his disciples. It is not, however, the humanist's uncritical, unqualified affirmation of the self, for it is heavily qualified by the acknowledgment of our own sinfulness. Christian believers are able to affirm only those aspects of the self which derive from our creation in God's image (e.g. our rationality, moral responsibility and capacity for love), while at the same time denying (that is, disowning and repudiating) all those aspects of the self which derive from the fall and from our own personal fallenness (e.g. our selfishness, covetousness, malice, hypocrisy and pride). These Christian forms of self-affirmation and self-denial are very far from being expressions of a preoccupation with ourselves, still less the current infatuation with the self. On the contrary, they are directed not towards self, but towards God.

They are part and parcel of our worship of God as our Creator and our Judge.

Yet some Christian writers have tried to argue that Christianity itself is about self-esteem, that we must give up concentrating on sin, guilt, judgment and atonement, that we must present salvation instead as the discovery of the self, and that the endorsement of the second commandment by Jesus was an implicit call to love ourselves as well as our neighbour. But this is not true at all. Self-love in Scripture is a synonym for sin, not the path to freedom. *Agapē*-love means the sacrifice of oneself in the service of others. By its very nature it cannot be self-directed. How can we sacrifice ourselves to serve ourselves? It is impossible. The very idea is a nonsense. The way of Jesus is the opposite. He taught the great paradox that only when we lose ourselves do we find ourselves, only when we die to ourselves do we learn to live, and only through serving others are we ourselves free. Or, to return to Paul in Galatians, only when we love do joy and peace follow. The self-conscious pursuit of happiness will always end in failure. But when we forget ourselves in the self-giving service of love, then joy and peace come flooding into our lives as incidental, unlooked-for blessings.

Love in action

Third, *love issues in action*. For if love is the first fruit of the Spirit, with joy and peace following in its wake, next come 'patience, kindness, goodness'. Love is not just romance, let alone eroticism. It is not even pure sentiment or emotion. It sounds abstract, but it leads to positive attitudes and concrete actions, namely 'patience', 'kindness' and 'goodness'. And, as I believe the Russian novelist Fyodor Dostoyevsky wrote, 'love in action is much more terrible than love in dreams'. For love is always seeking the true welfare of others, at whatever personal cost.

'Patience' is a negative quality. It is often translated 'long-suffering', for it describes patience with people rather than with circumstances. It includes forbearance towards those who are demanding or aggravating. It never forgets the 'immense patience' of Christ towards us.[22]

'Kindness' and 'goodness' are both positive qualities. The former is generosity of thought, *wishing* good to other people, while the latter is generosity of action, actually *doing* for them the good we wish them.

It seems right, then, to discern a progression in these three Christian graces. Patience endures the malice of others and refuses to retaliate. Kindness turns tolerance into kindliness, not wishing people ill, but wishing them well. And goodness converts the wish into the deed, taking the initiative to serve people in action.

All three qualities are characteristics and outworkings of love. For, as the apostle writes elsewhere, 'Love is patient, love is kind',[23] and we are to 'serve one another . . . in love'.[24] There is little value in making grand declarations of love for the human race; we have to get involved with real people in real situations. It is then that love's 'patience, kindness, goodness' will be put to the test.

Fourth, *love is balanced by self-control.* For 'the fruit of the Spirit is . . . faithfulness, gentleness and self-control'. These three qualities seem to be different nuances of the mastery of ourselves. 'Faithfulness' is reliability or trustworthiness in such areas as keeping our promises and fulfilling our undertakings. 'Gentleness' translates *prautēs*, which is often rendered 'meekness'. But it is not a compliant, spineless, unprincipled kind of meekness. It certainly means being gentle, humble and considerate towards other people, but this will often require us to tame our strengths and harness our energies. The third word 'self-control' is *egkrateia*, 'which expresses the power or lordship which one has either over oneself or over something'.[25] It includes disciplining our instincts, restraining our temper and our tongue, and curbing our passions.

Why must love be 'balanced' by self-control? Because love is self-giving, and self-giving and self-control complement one another. For how can we give ourselves until we have first learned to control ourselves? Our self has to be mastered before it can be offered in the service of others. It is surely significant, therefore, that the ninefold fruit of the Spirit begins with self-giving and ends with self-control.

Love is the fruit of the Spirit

The fifth truth which emerges from this great text is that the *love* we have been thinking about (pre-eminent, bringing joy and peace, issuing in action and balanced by self-control) is *the fruit of the Spirit*. In other words, it is the natural consequence of the supernatural work of the Holy Spirit within us.

In the context, Paul is drawing a contrast between 'the flesh' and 'the Spirit', between 'the works of the flesh' and 'the fruit of the Spirit'. We need to pause for some definitions. By 'flesh' he means neither the soft tissue of skin and muscle which covers our bony skeleton, nor the human body (a mistake people make when they talk of greed and sexual immorality as 'the sins of the flesh'). Instead, he is talking about our inherited, fallen, twisted nature with its bias towards evil, its corrupt desires and its selfish demands. It has been well said that if we rub out the last letter of the word 'flesh' and then read it backwards, we discover exactly what it is.

By 'Spirit' Paul means neither the breath which animates our body, nor the spiritual side of human beings in contrast to the material. Instead, he means the Holy Spirit himself, who enters our personality when we repent and trust in Jesus, and whose indwelling presence is the mark of Christian identity[26] and the secret of Christian holiness.

Here, then, are the two protagonists in the struggle which Paul describes. On the one hand, there is 'the flesh', our self-centred fallen nature, and on the other, 'the Spirit', the personal indwelling Spirit of God. Paul tells us three truths about the conflict between these forces.

First, the desires of the flesh and of the Spirit are *active* desires. 'For the sinful nature [i.e. 'the flesh'] desires what is contrary to the Spirit, and the Spirit what is contrary to the sinful nature. They are in conflict with each other.'[27] Thus, both the flesh and the Spirit have desires, which are alive, active, energetic and strong. The reason for stressing this is that throughout church history, perfectionist groups have taught that after the new birth our fallen nature is inert and inactive, even dead. But Scripture is not on their side. The command that we should 'not gratify the desires of the flesh',[28] and the statement that 'the sinful flesh desires what is contrary to the Spirit',[29] would both be nonsensical if our fallen nature no longer had any desires. No, the Christian life is one of unremitting conflict with the world, the flesh and the devil.

Second, the desires of the flesh and of the Spirit are *opposite* desires. A fierce antagonism exists between them. 'The desires of the flesh are against the Spirit, and the desires of the Spirit are against the flesh; for these are opposed to each other.'[30] As Bishop J. B. Lightfoot put it in his commentary on Galatians, 'Between the Spirit and the flesh there is not only no alliance; there is an interminable deadly feud.'[31]

Moreover, the contrary nature of the desires of the flesh and the Spirit are made plain in the contrast between 'the works of the flesh'[32] and 'the fruit of the Spirit'.[33] The former are very unpleasant. Paul lists fifteen of them. They seem to fall into four categories – sexual sins (immorality and licentiousness), religious sins (idolatry and sorcery, the latter being the secret attempt to steal divine or demonic power by magic), social sins (eight of them including malice, jealousy, temper, quarrelling and selfish ambition) and personal sins (drunkenness and orgies). It is an ugly catalogue of activities in which people assert themselves against God and others.

The ninefold fruit of the Spirit,[34] which we have already considered, presents a beautiful contrast. Indeed, it would be hard to imagine a greater contrast. For here is godliness instead of godlessness;

authentic joy and peace in place of the pursuit of sinful pleasure; kindness and goodness over against malice and envy; and self-control rather than self-indulgence.

Third, Paul insists that the desires of the flesh and of the Spirit are *controllable* desires. It is possible, he writes, for the Spirit to gain ascendancy over the flesh and subdue it, for love to triumph over selfishness, and for goodness to be victorious over evil. How? The secret lies in adopting the right attitude to both the flesh and the Spirit.

Our attitude to our fallen nature should be one of ruthless rejection. For 'those who belong to Christ Jesus have crucified the flesh with its passions and desires'.[35] We have taken this evil, slimy, slippery thing called 'the flesh' and nailed it to the cross. This was our initial repentance. Crucifixion is dramatic imagery for our uncompromising rejection of all known evil. Crucifixion does not lead to a quick or an easy death; it is an execution of lingering pain. Yet it is decisive; there is no possibility of escaping from it.

Our attitude to the Holy Spirit, on the other hand, is to be one of unconditional surrender. Paul uses several expressions for this. We are to 'live by the Spirit', to be 'led by the Spirit' and to 'keep in step with the Spirit'.[36] We are to allow him his rightful sovereignty over us, and follow his righteous promptings.

Thus, both our rejection of the flesh and our surrender to the Spirit need to be repeated daily, however decisive our original rejection and surrender may have been. In Jesus' words, we are to 'take up [our] cross daily' and follow him.[37] We are also to go on being filled with the Spirit,[38] as we open our personality to him daily. Both our rejection and our surrender are also to be worked out in disciplined habits of life. It is those who 'sow to the Spirit'[39] who reap the fruit of the Spirit. And to 'sow to the Spirit' means to cultivate the things of the Spirit. This means, for example, the wise use of the Lord's Day, the discipline of daily prayer and Bible reading, our regular worship and attendance at Communion or the Lord's Supper, the cultivation of our Christian friendships and our involvement in Christian service. An inflexible principle, in both the material and moral realms, is that we reap what we sow. The rule is invariable. It cannot be changed, for 'God cannot be mocked'.[40] We must not therefore be surprised if we do not reap the fruit of the Spirit when all the time we are sowing to the flesh. Did we think we could cheat or fool God?

To change the metaphor, I remember reading years ago of a visitor to the mountains of southern California. He met an old mountaineer, whose two dogs were continuously fighting. The visitor asked him which dog usually won. The mountaineer chewed his tobacco for a while in silence, and then replied, 'The one I feeds the most.' In the same way our new nature will gain the victory over the old only in so far as we feed the new and starve the old.

There is only one person, in the long history of the world, in whom the fruit of the Spirit has always ripened to perfection. That person is Jesus of Nazareth. Indeed, Paul's ninefold fruit may be seen as a portrait of Jesus Christ. For he loved as no-one else has ever loved, in laying down his life for his enemies. He spoke both of 'my joy' and of 'my peace'.[41] He was wonderfully patient with his dim-witted apostles. He was invariably kind and full of good works. He was also steadfastly reliable and always gentle, in fact 'gentle and humble in heart'.[42] And he had perfect self-control, so that 'when they hurled insults at him, he did not retaliate'.[43]

Dr Kenneth Moynagh, who worked for many years as a medical missionary at Matana in Burundi, once summarized the fruit of the Spirit, with its emphasis on love, in this way:

Joy is love exulting, and peace is love at rest;
Patience, love enduring in every trial and test.
Gentleness, love yielding to all that is not sin,
Goodness, love in actions that flow from Christ within.

Faith is love's eyes opened the living Christ to see;
Meekness, love not fighting, but bowed at Calvary.
Temperance, love in harness and under Christ's control,
For Christ is love in person, and love, Christ in the soul.

If the fruit of the Spirit is Christlikeness, Christlikeness is God's personal purpose for all his people.

- It is his *eternal* purpose, 'for those whom God foreknew he also predestined to be conformed to the image of his Son'.[44]
- It is his *historical* purpose, as 'we . . . are being transformed into his image with ever-increasing glory'.[45]
- It is his *eschatological* purpose, for, although 'what we will be has not yet been made known', nevertheless 'we know that when Christ appears, we shall be like him, for we shall see him as he is'.[46]

The only way to understand the disappointments and frustrations of life, the loneliness, the suffering and the pain, is to see them as part of our loving Father's discipline in his determination to make us like Christ.[47]

I am sometimes asked, perhaps in a newspaper, radio or television interview, whether at my age I have any ambitions left. I always now reply, 'Yes, my overriding ambition is (and, I trust, will be until I die) that I may become a little bit more like Christ.'

Reflection questions from Tim Chester

1 Which is the chief distinguishing mark of your church? What about your life? What could you do to ensure that love is the pre-eminent characteristic?
2 Which signs do you see of the pursuit of self-realization and self-esteem in the world around you? Why is this self-defeating?

3 Patience endures malice, kindness responds by wishing people well and goodness converts this wish into action. At which point does your love come unstuck? In which ways do you need to combine love with self-control?

4 Which practical steps could you take to reject everything that belongs to the flesh?

5 Which practical steps could you take to surrender to the Spirit and cultivate the things of the Spirit?

6 Can you think of a time when God used a disappointment or frustration to make you more Christlike?

Conclusion
The now and the not yet

I began in the Introduction with the tension between the 'then' (past) and the 'now' (present); I end with another tension, between the 'now' (present) and the 'not yet' (future). These two tensions belong together. For it is in and through Jesus Christ that the past, the present and the future are brought into a creative relationship. Christians live in the present, but do so in thankfulness for the past and in anticipation of the future.

As I conclude this book, I'm going to focus on balanced biblical Christianity. Balance is a rare commodity these days in almost every sphere, not least among us who seek to follow Christ.

One of the things about the devil is that he is a fanatic, and the enemy of all common sense, moderation and balance. One of his favourite pastimes is to tip Christians off balance. If he cannot get us to *deny* Christ, he will get us to *distort* Christ instead. As a result, lopsided Christianity is widespread, in which we overemphasize one aspect of a truth, while underemphasizing another.

A balanced grasp of the now–not-yet tension would be very beneficial for Christian unity, and especially to a greater harmony among evangelical believers. We may agree on the doctrinal and ethical fundamentals of the faith. Yet we seem to be constitutionally prone to quarrelling and dividing, or simply to going our own way and building our own empires.

Kingdom come and coming

Fundamental to New Testament Christianity is the perspective that we are living 'in between times' – between the first and the second comings of Christ, between kingdom come and kingdom coming.

The theological basis for this tension is to be found in Jesus' own teaching about the kingdom of God. Everyone accepts both that the kingdom featured prominently in his teaching and that he announced its coming. Where scholars have disagreed, however, is over the time of its arrival. Has the kingdom already come, because Jesus brought it with him? Or is its coming still in the future, so that we await it expectantly? Or does the truth lie between these positions?

Albert Schweitzer is an example of a scholar who thought that, according to Jesus, the kingdom lay entirely in the future. As an apocalyptic prophet, Jesus taught (mistakenly) that God was about to intervene supernaturally and establish his kingdom. The radical demands he made on his disciples were an 'interim ethic' in the light of the imminent arrival of the kingdom. Schweitzer's position is known as 'thoroughgoing' or 'consistent' eschatology.

At the opposite extreme was C. H. Dodd with his belief that the coming of the kingdom is wholly in the past (known as 'realized eschatology'). He laid a heavy emphasis on two verses whose verbs are in the perfect tense, namely 'The kingdom of God has arrived'[1] and 'The kingdom of God has come upon you.'[2] Dodd concluded that there is no future coming of the kingdom and that passages which speak of one were not part of Jesus' own teaching.

In place of these extreme polarities, most scholars have taken a middle position – that Jesus spoke of the kingdom as both a present reality and a future expectation.

Jesus clearly taught that the time of fulfilment had arrived;[3] that 'the strong man' was now bound and disarmed, enabling the plundering of his goods, as was evident from his exorcisms;[4] that the kingdom was already either 'within' or 'among' people;[5] and that it could now be 'entered' or 'received'.[6]

Yet the kingdom was a future expectation as well. It would not be perfected until the last day. So he looked forward to the end, and taught his disciples to do so also. They were to pray 'your kingdom come'[7] and to 'seek' it first,[8] giving priority to its expansion. At times he also referred to the final state of his followers in terms of 'entering' the kingdom[9] or 'receiving' it.[10]

One way in which the Bible expresses the tension between the 'now' and the 'not yet' is in the terminology of the two 'ages'. From the perspective of the Old Testament, history is divided between 'this present age' and 'the last days', namely the kingdom of righteousness to be introduced by the Messiah.[11] This simple structure of two consecutive ages was decisively changed, however, by the coming of Jesus. For he brought in the new age, and died for us in order to deliver us 'from the present evil age'.[12] As a result, the Father has already 'rescued us from the dominion of darkness and brought us into the kingdom of the Son he loves'.[13] We have even been raised from death and seated with Christ in the heavenly realm.[14]

At the same time, the old age persists. So the two ages overlap. 'The darkness is passing and the true light is already shining.' One day the old age will be terminated (which will be 'the end of the age'),[15] and the new age, which was introduced with Christ's first coming, will be brought about at his second. Meanwhile, the two ages continue, and we are caught in the tension between them. We are summoned not to 'conform to the pattern of this world', but rather to 'be transformed' according to God's will and to live consistently as children of the light.[16]

Nevertheless, the tension remains: we have already *been* saved, yet also we *shall* be saved one day.[17] And we are already God's adopted children, yet we also are waiting for our adoption.[18] Already we have 'crossed over from death to life', yet eternal life is also a future gift.[19] Already Christ is reigning, although his enemies have not yet become his footstool.[20]

Caught between the present and the future, the characteristic stance of Christians is variously described as hoping,[21] waiting,[22] longing,[23] and groaning,[24] as we wait both 'eagerly'[25] and also 'patiently'.[26]

The essence of the interim period between the 'now' and the 'not yet' is the presence of the Holy Spirit in the people of God. On the one hand, the gift of the Spirit is the distinctive blessing of the kingdom of God and the principal sign that the new age has dawned.[27] On the other, because his indwelling is only the beginning of our kingdom inheritance, it is also the guarantee that the rest will one day be ours. The New Testament uses three metaphors to illustrate this. The Holy Spirit is the 'firstfruits', pledging that the full harvest will follow,[28] the 'deposit' or first instalment, pledging that the full payment will be made,[29] and the foretaste, pledging that the full feast will one day be enjoyed.[30]

Here are some examples of the tension between the 'now' and the 'not yet'.

Revelation, holiness and healing

The first example is in *the intellectual sphere*, or the question of *revelation*.

We affirm with joyful confidence that God has revealed himself to human beings, not only in the created universe, in our reason and our conscience, but supremely in his Son Jesus Christ, and in the Bible's witness to him. We dare to say that we know God, because he has himself taken the initiative to draw aside the curtain which would otherwise hide him from us. We rejoice greatly that his Word throws light on our path.[31]

But we do not yet know God as he knows us. Our knowledge is partial because his revelation has been partial. He has revealed everything which he intends to reveal, and which he considers to be for our good, but not everything that there is to reveal. There are many mysteries left and so 'we live by faith, not by sight'.[32]

We should take our stand alongside those biblical authors who, although they knew themselves to be agents of divine revelation, nevertheless confessed humbly that their knowledge remained limited. Even Moses, 'whom the LORD knew face to face', acknowledged, 'O Sovereign LORD, you have only [RSV] begun to show to your servant your greatness and your strong hand.'[33] Then think of the apostle Paul, who likened his knowledge both to the immature thoughts of a child and to the distorted reflections of a mirror.[34]

So, then, although it is right to glory in the givenness and finality of God's revelation, it is also right to confess our ignorance of many things. We know and we don't know. 'The secret things belong to the LORD our God, but the things revealed belong to us and to our children for ever, that we may follow all the words of this law.'[35] It is very important to maintain this distinction. Speaking personally, I would like to see more boldness in our proclaiming what has been revealed, and more reticence about what has been kept secret. Agreement in plainly revealed truth is necessary for unity, even while we give each other freedom in secondary matters. And the way to recognize these is when Christians who are equally anxious to be submissive to Scripture nevertheless reach different conclusions about them. I am thinking, for example, about controversies over baptism, church government, liturgy and ceremonies, claims about spiritual gifts, and the fulfilment of prophecy.

The second tension is in *the moral sphere*, or the question of *holiness*.

God has already put his Holy Spirit within us, in order to make us holy.[36] The Holy Spirit is actively at work within us, subduing our fallen, selfish human nature and causing his fruit to ripen in our character, as we saw earlier.[37] Already, we can affirm, he is transforming us into the image of Christ.[38]

But our fallen nature has not been eradicated, for 'the flesh desires what is contrary to the Spirit',[39] so that 'if we claim to be without sin, we deceive ourselves'.[40] We have not yet become completely conformed to God's perfect will, for we do not yet love God with all our being, or our neighbour as ourselves. As Paul put it, we have 'not already become perfect' (GNT), but we 'press on towards the goal', confident that 'he who began a good work in [us] will carry it on to completion until the day of Christ Jesus'.[41]

So, then, we are caught in a painful tension between the 'now' and the 'not yet', between dismay over our continuing failures and the promise of ultimate freedom. On the one hand, we must take God's command, 'Be holy because I . . . am holy',[42] and Jesus' instruction, 'Go, and do not sin again',[43] with the utmost seriousness. On the other hand, we have to acknowledge the reality of indwelling sin alongside the reality of the indwelling Spirit.[44] The sinless perfection we long for continues to elude us.

The third tension between the 'already' and the 'not yet' is to be found in *the physical sphere* or the question of *healing*.

We affirm that the long-promised kingdom of God broke into history with Jesus Christ, who was not content merely to *proclaim* the kingdom, but went on to *demonstrate* its arrival by the extraordinary things he did. His power was especially evident in the human body as he healed the sick, expelled demons and raised the dead.

He also gave authority to both the Twelve and the Seventy to extend his mission in Israel, and to perform miracles. How much wider he intended his authority to go is a matter of dispute. Generally speaking, miracles were 'the signs of a true apostle'.[45] Nevertheless, it would be foolish to attempt to limit or domesticate God. We must allow him his freedom and his sovereignty, and be entirely open to the possibility of physical miracles today.

But God's kingdom has not yet come in its fullness. For 'the kingdom of the world' has not yet 'become the kingdom of our Lord and of his Christ' when 'he will reign for ever and ever'.[46] In particular, our bodies have not yet been redeemed and nature has not yet been entirely brought under Christ's rule.

So we have to recognize the 'already'–'not-yet' tension in this sphere too. To be sure, we have 'tasted . . . the powers of the coming age',[47] but so far it has been only a taste. Part of our Christian experience is that the resurrection life of Jesus is 'revealed in our mortal body'.[48] At the same time, our bodies remain frail and mortal. To claim perfect health now would be to anticipate our resurrection. The bodily resurrection of Jesus was the pledge, and indeed the beginning, of God's new creation. But God has not yet uttered the decisive word, 'I am making everything new!'[49] Those who dismiss the very possibility of miracles today forget the 'already' of the kingdom, while those who expect them as what has been called 'the normal Christian life' forget that the kingdom is 'not yet'.

Church and society

Fourth, the same tension is experienced in *the ecclesiastical sphere*, or the question of *church discipline*.

Jesus the Messiah is gathering round him a people of his own, a community characterized by the truth, love and holiness to which he has called it. But Christ has not yet presented his bride to himself 'as a radiant church, without stain or wrinkle or any other blemish, but holy and blameless'.[50] On the contrary, her present life and witness are marred by error, discord and sin.

So, then, whenever we think about the church, we need to hold together the ideal and the reality. The church is both committed to truth and prone to error, both united and divided, both pure and impure. Not that we are to accept its failures. We are to cherish the vision of both the doctrinal and ethical purity and the visible unity of the church. We are called to 'fight the good fight of the faith',[51] and to 'make every effort to keep the unity of the Spirit through the bond of peace'.[52] And in pursuit of these things there is a place for discipline in cases of serious heresy or sin.

And yet error and evil are not going to be eradicated completely from the church in this world. They will continue to coexist with truth and goodness. 'Let both grow together until the harvest,' Jesus said in the parable of the wheat and the weeds.[53] Neither the Bible nor church history justifies the use of severe disciplinary measures in an attempt to secure a perfectly pure church in this world.

The fifth area of tension between the 'now' and the 'then', the 'already' and the 'not yet', is *the social sphere*, or the question of *progress*.

We affirm that God is at work in human society. This is partly in his 'common grace', as he gives the world the blessings of family and government, by which evil is restrained and relationships are ordered. And it is also through the members of his redeemed community, who penetrate society like salt and light, making a difference by hindering decay and dispelling darkness.

But God has not yet created the promised 'new heaven and . . . new earth, where righteousness dwells'.[54] There are still 'wars and rumours of wars'.[55] Swords have not yet been beaten into ploughshares and spears into pruning hooks.[56] The nations have not yet renounced war as a method of settling their disputes. Selfishness, cruelty and fear continue.

So, then, although it is right to campaign for social justice and to expect to improve society further, we know that we shall never perfect it. Although we know the transforming power of the gospel and the wholesome effects of Christian salt and light, we also know that evil is ingrained in human nature and human society. Only Christ at his second coming will eradicate evil and enthrone righteousness for ever.

Here, then, are five areas (intellectual, moral, physical, ecclesiastical and social) in which it is vital to preserve the tension between the 'already' and the 'not yet'.

Three types of Christian

There are three distinct types of Christian, according to the extent to which they manage to maintain this biblical balance.

First, there are *the 'already' Christians* who emphasize what God has already given us in Christ. But they give the impression that, in consequence, there are now no mysteries left, no sins that cannot be overcome, no diseases that cannot be healed, and no evils that cannot be eradicated. In short, they seem to believe that perfection is attainable now.

Their motives are blameless. They want to glorify Christ – so they refuse to set limits to what he is able to do. But their optimism can easily degenerate into presumption and end up in disillusion. They forget the 'not yet' of the New Testament, and that perfection awaits the second coming of Christ.

Second, there are *the 'not-yet' Christians* who emphasize the incompleteness for the time being of the work of Christ and look forward to the time when he will complete what he has begun. But they seem to be preoccupied with our human ignorance and failure, the pervasive reign of disease and death, and the impossibility of securing either a pure church or a perfect society.

Their motive is excellent too. If the 'already' Christians want to glorify Christ, the 'not-yet' Christians want to humble sinners. They are determined to be true to the Bible in their emphasis on our human depravity. But their pessimism can easily degenerate into complacency; it can also lead to acceptance of the status quo and to apathy in the face of evil. They forget the 'already' of what Christ has done by his death, resurrection and gift of the Spirit – and of what he can do in our lives, and in church and society, as a result.

Third, there are *the 'already–not-yet' Christians*. They want to give equal weight to the two comings of Jesus. On the one hand, they have great confidence in the 'already', in what God has said and done through Christ. On the other hand, they exhibit a genuine humility before the 'not yet', humility to confess that the world will remain fallen and half-saved until Christ perfects at his second coming what he began at his first.

It is this combination of the 'already' and the 'not yet' which characterizes authentic biblical evangelicalism, and which exemplifies the balance that is so urgently needed today.

Our position as 'contemporary Christians' rests securely on the person of Jesus, whose death and resurrection belong to the 'already' of the past and whose glorious second coming to the 'not yet' of the future. As we acclaim in faith and triumph:

Christ has died!
Christ is risen!
Christ will come again!

Notes

Preface
1 Revelation 1:8.
2 Hebrews 13:8.

Series introduction: the Contemporary Christian – the then and the now
1 Psalm 119:105; cf. 2 Peter 1:19.
2 Dietrich Bonhoeffer, *Letters and Papers from Prison*, enlarged edn (SCM Press, 1971), p. 279.
3 Matthew 11:19.
4 See Jaroslav Pelikan, *Jesus Through the Centuries* (Yale University Press, 1985), pp. 182–193.
5 2 Corinthians 11:4.
6 2 Timothy 1:15; cf. 4:11, 16.
7 Acts 26:25.
8 Ezekiel 2:6–7.

1 The listening ear
1 James 3:8.
2 James 1:19–20.
3 See Alan E. Nourse, *The Body* (Time Life, 1968); also two books by Paul Brand and Philip Yancey entitled *In His Image* (Hodder & Stoughton, 1984) and *Fearfully and Wonderfully Made* (Hodder & Stoughton, 1981).
4 Deuteronomy 30:20.
5 Psalm 95:7 (rv).
6 Jeremiah 13:10; cf. Isaiah 30:9.
7 Zechariah 7:13; cf. Jeremiah 21:10–11.
8 Genesis 22:1.

9 1 Samuel 3:4, 6, 8, 10.

10 Acts 9:3–7.

11 Exodus 33:11.

12 Deuteronomy 34:10.

13 John 10:3–5.

14 Ephesians 2:20.

15 Matthew 7:16; 1 Thessalonians 5:20–22.

16 Hebrews 4:12.

17 Ephesians 6:17.

18 E.g. Luke 10:26.

19 E.g. Matthew 19:4; 21:42.

20 E.g. Romans 4:3; Galatians 4:30.

21 E.g. Revelation 2:7.

22 1 Samuel 3:9–10.

23 Isaiah 50:4.

24 Luke 10:39.

25 Luke 10:42.

26 Proverbs 12:15; cf. 13:10; 15:12, 22; 20:18.

27 Proverbs 15:31; cf. 9:8; 17:10; 25:12; 27:5.

28 Proverbs 18:15.

29 Proverbs 1:8.

30 *Reader's Digest*, September 1937.

31 Ibid., p. xv.

32 Stephen B. Oates, *Abraham Lincoln: The Man Behind the Myths* (New American Library, 1984), pp. 125–126.

33 See e.g. *Evangelism and Social Responsibility: An Evangelical Commitment*, known as 'The Grand Rapids Report' (Paternoster, 1982), especially pp. 5–7.

34 Dietrich Bonhoeffer, *Life Together* (Harper and Brothers, 1954), pp. 97–99.

35 Proverbs 18:13.

36 From a paper entitled 'Presence and Proclamation', read at a European Consultation on Mission Studies in April, 1968.

37 M. A. C. Warren, *Crowded Canvas* (Hodder & Stoughton, 1974), pp. 16, 18.

38 Proverbs 12:16.

39 Proverbs 21:13.

2 Mind and emotions

1 Mark 12:30.

2 Romans 12:2; Ephesians 4:23.

3 E.g. Ephesians 4:26; 1 Peter 1:22.

4 Acts 24:16.

5 E.g. Matthew 6:10; Mark 14:36; Colossians 4:12.

6 1 Corinthians 14:20.

7 Lesslie Newbigin, *Foolishness to the Greeks* (SPCK, 1986), p. 70.

8 D. Martyn Lloyd-Jones, *The Christian Warfare* (Banner of Truth, 1976), p. 114.

9 2 Corinthians 5:7.

10 H. L. Mencken, who wrote for the *Baltimore Sun* and was sometimes called 'the sage of Baltimore'.

11 1 Corinthians 2:1–5.

12 Acts 18:4.

13 Acts 19:9–10.

14 Acts 26:25.

15 Philippians 1:7.

16 Chaim Potok, *The Chosen* (1967; Penguin 1970).

17 Ibid., p. 200.

18 Ibid., p. 273.

19 Ibid., p. 274.

20 Ibid., p. 277.

21 E.g. Hosea 11:8–9.

22 Romans 5:5.

23 Romans 8:15–16.

24 1 John 3:1.

25 1 Peter 1:8.

26 Romans 8:22–25; 2 Corinthians 5:2–4.

27 2 Corinthians 5:19–20.

28 E.g. Acts 20:19, 31; Philippians 3:18.

29 D. Martyn Lloyd-Jones, *Preaching and Preachers* (Hodder & Stoughton, 1971), p. 97.

30 1 Corinthians 15:26.

31 Cf. Mark 14:5.

32 B. B. Warfield, *The Person and Work of Christ* (Presbyterian & Reformed, 1950), pp. 115–117.

33 Bob Geldof with Paul Vallely, *Is That It?* (Penguin, 1986), p. 269.

34 Ibid., p. 271.

35 Ibid., p. 386.

36 Ephesians 4:26.

37 Galatians 5:19–21.

38 Luke 24:32.

39 Quoted by Ralph G. Turnbull in *A Minister's Obstacles* (1946; Baker, 1972), p. 97.

40 2 Corinthians 5:14.

3 Guidance, vocation and ministry

1 Ephesians 2:10.

2 Ephesians 5:17.

3 Colossians 1:9.

4 Colossians 4:12.

5 Romans 8:29.

6 Psalm 25:9.

7 Matthew 7:7; James 4:2.

8 Proverbs 13:10.

9 Psalm 32:8–9.

10 Matthew 2:13.

11 E.g. Galatians 5:8; 1 Peter 1:15.

12 E.g. Romans 8:28; Hebrews 9:15.

13 Romans 1:6.

14 1 Peter 3:9.

15 1 Corinthians 1:9.

16 Mark 3:14.

17 John 17:3.

18 Galatians 5:13.

19 Colossians 3:15.

20 1 Corinthians 1:2.

21 Romans 1:7 (RSV).

22 E.g. 1 Peter 1:15; 1 Thessalonians 4:7; 2 Timothy 1:9.

23 1 Peter 2:9.

24 1 Peter 2:20–21.

25 John 15:18, 20.

26 Hebrews 3:1; cf. Philippians 3:14.

27 1 Peter 5:10.

28 Romans 8:17.

29 Ephesians 4:1.

30 1 Corinthians 7:20.

31 1 Corinthians 7:20, 17.

32 1 Corinthians 7:17, 20, 24.

33 2 Corinthians 5:17.

34 1 Corinthians 7:14.

35 1 Corinthians 7:21.

36 Martin Luther, *Weimarer Ausgabe* (1883), vol. 44, pp. 130–131.

37 *Weimarer Ausgabe*, vol. 52, p. 124.

38 *Weimarer Ausgabe*, vol. 46, p. 166.

39 John Calvin, *Institutes*, III.x.6.

40 William Perkins, *A Treatise of the Vocations or Callings of Men*
in *The Work of William Perkins*, Courtenay Library of Reformation
Classics, ed. Ian Breward (Sutton Courtenay Press, 1970),
p. 458.

41 Cotton Mather, *A Christian at His Calling* (1701), p. 37.

42 Ibid., pp. 37–38.

43 See *The Willowbank Report: Gospel and Culture*, especially ch. 6, 'Wanted: Humble Messengers of the Gospel' (Lausanne Committee for World Evangelization, 1978).

44 Matthew 7:11.

45 Romans 12:2.

4 The first fruit of the Spirit

1 Galatians 5:22–23.

2 1 Timothy 6:12.

3 1 Timothy 6:20, literally; cf. 2 Timothy 1:14.

4 2 Thessalonians 2:15.

5 Jude 3.

6 1 Corinthians 13:2.

7 1 Corinthians 8:1.

8 Romans 3:28.

9 Luther's *Commentary on the Epistle to the Galatians* (1531; James Clarke, 1953), pp. 101, 143.

10 From the 'Sermon on Salvation' in the *First Book of Homilies* (1547).

11 R. T. Beckwith, G. E. Duffield and J. I. Packer, *Across the Divide* (Lyttleton Press, 1977), p. 58.

12 1 Corinthians 13:2.

13 1 Peter 1:8 (RSV).

14 Philippians 3:8.

15 1 Corinthians 13:1–2.

16 1 John 3:17.

17 1 Corinthians 13:3 (RSV).

18 1 John 4:8, 16.

19 1 John 4:19.

20 Dr Paul Vitz, *Psychology as Religion* (Eerdmans, 1977).

21 David Wells, *No Place for Truth* (Eerdmans, 1996).

22 1 Timothy 1:16.

23 1 Corinthians 13:4.

24 Galatians 5:13.

25 From the article on *egkrateia* by Walter Grundmann in *TDNT* 2 (1964).

26 Romans 8:9.

27 Galatians 5:17.

28 Galatians 5:16.

29 Galatians 5:17.

30 Galatians 5:17 (RSV).

31 J. B. Lightfoot, *Galatians* (1865), p. 209.

32 Galatians 5:19–21.

33 Galatians 5:22–23.

34 Galatians 5:22–23.

35 Galatians 5:24.

36 Galatians 5:16, 18, 25.

37 Luke 9:23.

38 Ephesians 5:18.

39 Galatians 6:8 (RSV).

40 Galatians 6:7.

41 E.g. John 15:11; 14:27.

42 Matthew 11:29.

43 1 Peter 2:23.

44 Romans 8:29.

45 2 Corinthians 3:18.

46 1 John 3:2.

47 E.g. Hebrews 12:4–11.

Conclusion: the now and the not yet

1 Mark 1:15, as he translates *ēngiken*.

2 Matthew 12:28, *ephthasen*.

3 E.g. Matthew 13:16–17; Mark 1:14–15.

4 Matthew 12:28–29; cf. Luke 10:17–18.

5 Luke 17:20–21.

6 E.g. Mark 10:15.

7 Matthew 6:10.

8 Matthew 6:33.

9 Mark 9:47; cf. Matthew 8:11.

10 Matthew 25:34.

11 E.g. Isaiah 2:2; Matthew 12:32; Mark 10:30.

12 Galatians 1:4.

13 Colossians 1:13; cf. Acts 26:18; 1 Peter 2:9.

14 Ephesians 2:6; Colossians 3:1.

15 E.g. Matthew 13:39; 28:20.

16 Romans 12:2; 13:11–14; 1 Thessalonians 5:4–8.

17 Romans 8:24; 5:9–10; 13:11.

18 Romans 8:15, 23.

19 John 5:24; 11:25–26; Romans 8:10–11.

20 Psalm 110:1; Ephesians 1:22; Hebrews 2:8.

21 Romans 8:24.

22 Philippians 3:20–21; 1 Thessalonians 1:9–10.

23 Romans 8:19.

24 Romans 8:22–23, 26; 2 Corinthians 5:2, 4.

25 Romans 8:23; 1 Corinthians 1:7.

26 Romans 8:25.

27 E.g. Isaiah 32:15; 44:3; Ezekiel 39:29; Joel 2:28; Mark 1:8;
   Hebrews 6:4–5.

28 Romans 8:23.

29 2 Corinthians 5:5; Ephesians 1:14.

30 Hebrews 6:4–5.

31 Psalm 119:105.

32 2 Corinthians 5:7.

33 Deuteronomy 34:10; cf. Numbers 12:8; Deuteronomy 3:24.

34 1 Corinthians 13:9–12.

35 Deuteronomy 29:29.

36 1 Thessalonians 4:7–8.

37 Galatians 5:16–26.

38 2 Corinthians 3:18.

39 Galatians 5:17.

40 1 John 1:8.

41 Philippians 3:12–14; 1:6.

42 E.g. Leviticus 19:2.

43 John 8:11 (RSV).

44 E.g. Romans 7:17, 20; 8:9, 11.

45 2 Corinthians 12:12 (RSV).

46 Revelation 11:15.

47 Hebrews 6:5.

48 2 Corinthians 4:10–11.

49 Revelation 21:5.

50 Ephesians 5:27; cf. Revelation 21:2.

51 1 Timothy 6:12.

52 Ephesians 4:3.

53 Matthew 13:30.

54 2 Peter 3:13; Revelation 21:1.

55 Mark 13:7.

56 Isaiah 2:4.

Enjoyed this book? Read the rest of the series.

Presenting John Stott's classic volume in five individual parts for today's audiences, the Contemporary Christian series has been sensitively modernized and updated by Tim Chester but retains the original core, clear and crucial Bible teaching.

The Gospel
978 1 78359 928 8

The Disciple
978 1 78359 930 1

The Bible
978 1 78359 770 3

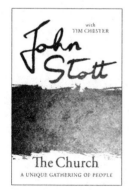

The Church
978 1 78359 924 0

The World
978 1 78359 926 4